NEW DIRECTIONS FOR EVALUATION
A Publication of the American Evaluation Association

Lois-ellin G. Datta, *Datta Analysis*
EDITOR-IN-CHIEF

Evaluating Initiatives to Integrate Human Services

Jules M. Marquart
Vanderbilt University

Ellen L. Konrad
Arizona Department of Economic Security

EDITORS

Number 69, Spring 1996

JOSSEY-BASS PUBLISHERS
San Francisco

EVALUATING INITIATIVES TO INTEGRATE HUMAN SERVICES
Jules M. Marquart, Ellen L. Konrad (eds.)
New Directions for Evaluation, no. 69
Lois-ellin G. Datta, Editor-in-Chief

ISSN 0164-7989   ISBN 0-7879-9903-2

NEW DIRECTIONS FOR EVALUATION is part of The Jossey-Bass Education
Series and is published quarterly by Jossey-Bass Inc., Publishers, 350
Sansome Street, San Francisco, California 94104-1342.

Subscriptions for 1996 cost $59.00 for individuals and $87.00 for institutions, agencies, and libraries.

EDITORIAL CORRESPONDENCE should be addressed to the Editor-in-Chief,
Lois-ellin G. Datta, P.O. Box 383768, Waikoloa, HI 96738.

Manufactured in the United States of America. Nearly all Jossey-Bass
books, jackets, and periodicals are printed on recycled paper that contains
at least 50 percent recycled waste, including 10 percent postconsumer
waste. Many of our materials are also printed with vegetable-based inks;
during the printing process, these inks emit fewer volatile organic com-
pounds (VOCs) than petroleum-based inks. VOCs contribute to the formation of smog.

EDITORIAL POLICY AND PROCEDURES

NEW DIRECTIONS FOR EVALUATION, a quarterly sourcebook, is an official publication of the American Evaluation Association. The journal publishes empirical, methodological, and theoretical works on all aspects of evaluation and related fields. Substantive areas may include any program, field, or issue with which evaluation is concerned, such as government performance, tax policy, energy, environment, mental health, education, job training, medicine, and public health. Also included are such topics as product evaluation, personnel evaluation, policy analysis, and technology assessment. In all cases, the focus on evaluation is more important than the substantive topics. We are particularly interested in encouraging a diversity of evaluation perspectives and experiences and in expanding the boundaries of our field beyond the evaluation of social programs.

The editors do not consider or publish unsolicited single manuscripts. Each issue of the journal is devoted to a single topic, with contributions solicited, organized, reviewed, and edited by a guest editor. Issues may take any of several forms, such as a series of related chapters, a debate, or a long article followed by brief critical commentaries. In all cases, the proposals must follow a specific format, which can be obtained from the editor-in-chief. These proposals are sent to members of the editorial board and to relevant substantive experts for peer review. The process may result in acceptance, a recommendation to revise and resubmit, or rejection. However, the editors are committed to working constructively with potential guest editors to help them develop acceptable proposals.

Lois-ellin G. Datta, Editor-in-Chief
P.O. Box 383768
Waikoloa, HI 96738

Jennifer C. Greene, Associate Editor
Department of Human Service Studies
Cornell University
Ithaca, NY 14853-4401

Gary Henry, Associate Editor
Public Administration and Urban Studies
Georgia State University
Atlanta, GA 30302-4039

CONTENTS

EDITORS' NOTES   1
Jules M. Marquart, Ellen L. Konrad

1. A Multidimensional Framework for Conceptualizing Human   5
Services Integration Initiatives
Ellen L. Konrad
A brief history of services integration efforts is presented and a framework
is provided that identifies key components of services integration projects
and how they may vary by degree of integration.

2. Methodological Issues in Evaluating Integrated Services Initiatives 21
Michael S. Knapp
Conceptualization and design issues are discussed along with promising and
less promising approaches to evaluation of integrated services initiatives.

3. Evaluating the 1992 and 1993 Community Integrated Service   35
System Projects
Richard N. Roberts, Barbara H. Wasik
The evaluation of a national, multisite services integration effort presented
challenges related to extreme variability across projects in the target population, strategies used to create integrated service systems, and the focus of
the intervention.

4. Evaluating a Statewide School-Linked Services Initiative: 51
California's Healthy Start
Mary M. Wagner, Deanna S. Gomby
The need for rigorous evaluation design must be balanced by the political,
policy, fiscal, and logistical realities of complex, diverse, and mutable ser-
vices integration projects.

5. Evaluation of State-Level Integrated Services Initiatives: 69
Colorado's Experience
Donna M. Garnett, Marsha S. Gould
A synthesis of evaluation lessons from two state-level services integration
efforts is presented; one initiative focuses on state-level policy changes
among state agencies and a second supports community-level system integration.

6. Implications for the Future of Service Delivery System Reform   85
William A. Morrill
A broader conceptualization of services integration in the context of service delivery system reform is suggested, and ways of better integrating policy, program development, and evaluation are discussed.

INDEX   97

EDITORS' NOTES

Our country is again in a sweep of efforts to integrate human services on the federal, state, and local levels. The initiatives of this decade represent the third generation of such efforts, beginning with federal initiatives started by former Health, Education, and Welfare secretary Elliot Richardson in the early 1970s, and continuing with renewed efforts in the 1980s during the Reagan and Bush administrations. State and, increasingly, local initiatives have followed suit.

Today's efforts stem from several sets of motives. First is a concern with the increasing fragmentation of services, which makes appropriate access difficult and stable support for service agencies uncertain. A second motive is a philosophical reorientation in human services that regards the family, not the individual, as the unit of service. The individual's behavior is perceived to be determined by the structure of the family in which she or he is embedded; the family is, in turn, affected by the structure, barriers, and influences of the community and the culture. This ecological theoretical approach suggests that if services are to be effective, they require closer coordination than currently exists. A third set of motives derives from the desire to reduce the costs of services, and the belief that improved efficiency in service delivery would, at the very least, reduce administrative costs. Programs based on each of these sets of motives are in process.

Yet it seems that the programmatic lessons of these efforts, much less what has been learned about their subsequent evaluation, have not been adequately examined. Each generation of services integration efforts, and sometimes each individual program, has to a certain extent reinvented the wheel instead of building on traditions of lessons learned about effective practices.

The impetus for this volume originated at a session on evaluating services integration efforts organized by the two editors at the 1993 American Evaluation Association (AEA) conference. We, along with our copresenter Frank Mondeaux and members of the audience, found that we all had confronted similar issues in designing and implementing the evaluations of very disparate services integration programs in different parts of the country. This volume represents an attempt to define the conceptual and methodological issues in the evaluation of integrated services systems and to begin to synthesize some of those lessons to improve evaluation practice.

The volume is organized around two introductory chapters that provide a framework for conceptual and methodological issues, followed by case study

Preparation of this volume was partially supported by the U.S. Department of Education, Early Education Programs for Children with Disabilities (Grant #H024K40004). We gratefully acknowledge the assistance of Dolly Gerregano in the preparation of this manuscript.

examples of three different evaluations. The case studies represent one federal-level and two state-level program evaluations. Although space did not permit the inclusion of a local program example, the cases presented here do cut across the fields of health, education, and social services. The authors of these chapters focus, in particular, on the evaluation lessons learned in their projects. The final chapter discusses implications for program and policy development and for further evaluation of services integration efforts.

Chapter One lays the foundation for the volume with a multidimensional framework for conceptualizing human services integration initiatives. Ellen L. Konrad presents a brief history of services integration efforts and proposes a broad definition of the topic. Her framework identifies the key components of services integration projects and posits that each component varies in the degree to which it is integrated.

In Chapter Two, Michael S. Knapp explains issues confronting evaluation of integrated services initiatives and argues that evaluation studies must be strongly conceptualized, descriptive, comparative, constructively skeptical, positioned from the bottom up, and collaborative. He offers some promising evaluation approaches to address those concerns and also suggests approaches that are unlikely to yield useful results.

In Chapter Three, Richard N. Roberts and Barbara H. Wasik present the design for evaluating a national, multisite initiative focusing on maternal and child health programs. They discuss an initial process study that describes program implementation across forty-one local sites and highlight the particular challenges in evaluating programs with extreme variability in target population, strategies used to create integrated service systems, and the focus of the intervention.

Chapter Four reviews the evaluation of the largest statewide school-linked services integration effort in the country. Mary M. Wagner and Deanna S. Gomby describe how they balanced the need for rigorous evaluation design with the political, policy, fiscal, and logistical realities of complex, diverse, and mutable projects.

In Chapter Five, Donna M. Garnett and Marsha S. Gould present the evaluations of two concurrent state-level services integration efforts: one that focuses on state-level policy changes among state agencies and one that supports community-level system integration through family resource centers. They discuss the policy context for the two initiatives and provide a synthesis of how the two studies inform program development and evaluation practice.

In Chapter Six, William A. Morrill argues that we should move from a focus on services integration efforts to the broader context of reform of the human services delivery system. He describes four policy objectives for service system reform, presents major methodological issues for evaluation, and recommends approaches for further evaluation work.

Although we were unable to include a chapter on local project initiatives, we have learned a number of lessons from our own experiences with services integration efforts that are worth highlighting in this discussion. Several of these lessons echo themes presented in the federal- and state-level case study chapters. One of the primary lessons is the importance of developing realistic expectations about the evaluation, especially given the complexity of these projects and the typically limited amount of evaluation funding available at the local level. Another word of advice is to anticipate the evolutionary nature of projects and recognize that in addition to the inherent instability of this intervention, such projects also tend to jump onto the bandwagon of every reform initiative that comes along. The result is that multiple reform efforts may occur simultaneously at the same site.

Especially true of smaller-scale projects is the need to find creative solutions to the intractable problems of connecting data systems for which existing ties are virtually nonexistent, such as developing low-cost ways to establish linkage and tracking capabilities. Another lesson that should not be overlooked (although some would argue otherwise) is the value of developing comparison populations, provided the sources and costs are reasonable. We also encourage taking advantage of collaborative evaluation through the pooling of cross-agency or cross-discipline evaluator resources. The benefits should include a more comprehensive perspective and a possible reduction in individual partner costs. Finally, because evaluators are truly on the front line in local projects, they may not be able to avoid becoming embroiled in the crossfire of local project politics. In serving the interests of multiple partners and stakeholders, it is more likely that evaluators will either be caught in disputes such as funding conflicts between sponsoring agencies and service providers or see results ignored (especially if the findings are negative).

Clearly, services integration initiatives provide new challenges and create new opportunities for program evaluation. The presence of multiple stakeholder groups highlights the need to use stakeholder and participatory approaches that acknowledge the sociopolitical, fiscal, and multidisciplinary realities of these efforts. These initiatives entail potentially expanded roles for evaluators because of the challenges of simultaneously addressing the evaluation concerns of policy makers, program managers, service providers, and consumers.

Further work is needed in developing the program theory of services integration that makes explicit its underlying assumptions and develops linkages between the social and human problems they are designed to address, the program components as implemented, and outcomes on the individual, family, community, and service system levels.

Finally, we encourage the use of a developmental approach to evaluate services integration initiatives. These programs rarely are implemented exactly as planned; by intent, they should be flexible and responsive to changing needs and the local context. Therefore, it seems more realistic to begin thinking of an evaluation design that proceeds in stages, initially carefully documenting the program development and constructing a management information system to capture baseline data on participant characteristics and service use, and then following the evolution of the program over time. As the initiative becomes established, it would be possible to refine program theory and to identify likely outcomes on the multiple levels of interest. Mixed-methods approaches are most appropriate in implementing such multistage, developmental evaluations.

Jules M. Marquart
Ellen L. Konrad
Editors

JULES M. MARQUART is research assistant professor at Vanderbilt University and research coordinator of the Early Childhood Research Institute on Inclusion.

ELLEN L. KONRAD is manager of the Office of Evaluation in the Arizona Department of Economic Security.

The ability to define and understand the "black box" of human services integration initiatives is aided by a multidimensional, multilevel framework.

A Multidimensional Framework for Conceptualizing Human Services Integration Initiatives

Ellen L. Konrad

Definition of Services Integration

Human services integration (SI) initiatives are, by their nature, complex approaches to service provision. They consist of multiple partners, operate along numerous dimensions and at various levels of intensity, and encompass a variety of components, structures, and designs. Like other multifaceted human services programs, and even more so than traditional categorical programs, they present particular challenges for evaluators (Weiss and Halpern, 1990).

In recent years, as discussion in the human services delivery field has shifted from the accomplishments of localized efforts to the prospects of "going to scale" with more global, systemic changes, there have also been calls for a new evaluation paradigm and new evaluation methodologies (Bruner, 1993). Therefore, an assessment and understanding of what has been learned about SI projects and their evaluations so far can provide a valuable backdrop for the exploration and development of new evaluation approaches.

Before beginning that discussion, it is important to provide some definition: given the seemingly infinite diversity of services integration initiatives,

---

The author wishes to thank Jules Marquart for editorial assistance and support in the preparation of this manuscript, Frank Mondeaux and Susan Labin for their helpful comments during the conceptualization of these ideas, and Irving Lazar for sharing some of his early unpublished remarks on services integration.

what do we mean by that term? Are there specific characteristics of SI efforts or parameters for defining them, and what is their purpose? What types of efforts should be included? What should not? Does information sharing between two separate agencies qualify as service integration? What about two entirely separate programs located adjacent to one another that are administratively part of the same agency?

The literature is replete with somewhat different definitions of human services integration. Examples of key sources come from the Department of Health and Human Services, the U.S. General Accounting Office, the National Center for Service Integration, and the National Center for Children in Poverty. All are somewhat similar to the following, which we propose as a general definition for this volume: human services integration is a process by which two or more entities establish linkages for the purpose of improving outcomes for needy people. For the purposes of discussing the evaluation of SI efforts, we believe it is important to keep the definition of *services integration* as broad and inclusive as possible.

Integrated services are distinguished from traditional categorical programs, which tend to be targeted to specific populations with unique funding and eligibility requirements. Typically, each program has its own constituencies, legislation, specifications, and regulations, and there are no mechanisms to link separate programs. Further, nonintegrated services are generally characterized as being unnecessarily problematic to clients, duplicative, fragmented, expensive, inefficient, unresponsive, unaccountable, crisis oriented, and steeped in professional interests rather than the best interests of clients (Martin, Chackerian, Imershein, and Frumkin, 1983).

The impetus for services integration initiatives, then, is based on the assumption that existing human service delivery systems are seriously deficient and that some form of coordination or consolidation is necessary for their improvement. The benefits of SI projects are purported to include, but are not limited to, the ability to address the needs of multiproblem clients in a comprehensive manner, greater service accessibility and continuity, early intervention and prevention, reduced duplication, reduced waste and inefficiency, reduced costs, and greater accountability (Wingspread Conference, 1993).

Brief History of Services Integration Initiatives

Although the history of SI initiatives has been described in detail elsewhere (Kusserow, 1991a; Kagan, 1993; Kagan, Goffin, Golub, and Pritchard, 1995), a synopsis may be helpful here to provide a context and foundation for the chapters that follow.

The 1970s. Early in the decade, former U.S. Department of Health, Education and Welfare (HEW) secretary Elliot Richardson took a strong lead in calling for reforms in the social service delivery system that would break down categorical barriers and integrate services across program areas. Throughout the 1970s, HEW and later its successor agency, the Department of Health and

Human Services (HHS), began a series of initiatives to promote the integration of human services.

One of the initial coordination efforts during this era was in the area of programs for young children. Kagan recounts that "the *Community Coordinated Child Care (4C)* program was launched in 1971 to coordinate early child care and education services in communities nationwide by encouraging local programs to share staff and services and engage in activities such as cross-training" (Kagan, Goffin, Golub, and Pritchard, 1995, p. 6).

In 1972, in an effort to increase the body of information about service integration efforts, HEW funded forty-five Services Integration Targets of Opportunity (SITO) research projects. Most of these projects consisted of comprehensive service delivery efforts carried out by state or local governments or private agencies. They were intended to provide replicable information on how to integrate the delivery of a wide range of human services and provide documentation about what happened as a result.

Another HEW initiative in the mid 1970s awarded grants for Comprehensive Human Services Planning and Delivery Systems (CHSPDS) to five local communities. CHSPDS projects were designed to develop and field-test models for local comprehensive planning, delivery, and management of social services; to develop methods for generating accurate data bases; and to evaluate their impact on the effectiveness and efficiency of the service delivery system. All grantees were required to develop common data bases using a common set of definitions, recipient goals, and cost-accounting systems. The projects faced major funding reductions in the final year and a planned overall evaluation was never conducted.

The 1980s. By the late 1970s and early 1980s, HEW's SI efforts began losing momentum as repeated attempts to pass substantial SI legislation failed in Congress due to widespread opposition by categorical program interest groups. As a result, the SI agenda fell increasingly to state and local governments, who were spurred on by passage of federal social services block grants in 1975 and 1981. However, enthusiasm for block grants also began to wane by the mid 1980s, when a downturn in the national economy and subsequent funding shortfalls outweighed the advantages of decategorization and increased flexibility.

The Deficit Reduction Act of 1984 authorized federally funded Services Integration Pilot Projects (SIPPs) through the reconstituted Department of Health and Human Services to demonstrate the use of integrated service delivery systems as a means of helping people to achieve social and economic self-sufficiency. The HHS Office of Human Development Services selected five states for multiyear projects beginning in 1985. Each state had a one-year planning period, followed by a two-year implementation phase. Although each of the five states focused on different target populations, they shared two common characteristics: each state used a client-centered case management approach to service delivery, where each client's needs were assessed, service plans developed, services delivered or facilitated, and follow-up provided; and each state conducted its own evaluation of its project, and the federal office contracted for an independent evaluation to analyze project outcomes in each state and across states. Due to the initial evaluation contractor's financial difficulties, the overall evaluation was not completed until early 1994.

By the end of the 1980s, SI projects increasingly involved integration within categorical programs and for specific target groups. For example, the Interagency Low-Income Opportunity Advisory Board, established by executive order in 1987, facilitated the coordination of public assistance programs and policies across federal agencies and other levels of government, and became a focal point for early welfare reform demonstration proposals.

1990 to the Present. The past few years have seen a resurgence in SI projects at all jurisdictional levels and across many disciplines. Although federal agencies still fund large-scale projects, they are no longer the driving force. States and localities have taken the lead. SI initiatives are proliferating in such areas as wraparound mental health services, family preservation and support services, services for at-risk children and youth, and one-stop employment and training centers. The projects described in Chapters Three, Four, and Five of this volume are but three examples of current SI efforts at the federal and state levels.

The federal role has also shifted and expanded somewhat as HHS has entered into partnerships with private foundations to provide technical assistance to those implementing service integration efforts. A major source of such assistance is the National Center for Service Integration, a consortium of six organizations that serves as a resource for programs and organizations and an information clearinghouse of documents on service integration efforts. Also, various interdisciplinary gatherings such as the Family Impact Seminars in 1991 and 1993 and the Wingspread Conference in 1993 have been held to focus on the state of the art in services integration and to raise related research and evaluation issues.

A growing number of SI projects are school-based or school-linked. Increasingly, educators and policy makers are finding it difficult to achieve education goals because of the socioeconomic and related problems faced by students and their families (see Chapter Four, this volume). In many areas of the country teachers complain that children do not come to school ready to learn and, as a result, teachers do as much social work as they do teaching.

Those concerns have created a receptive climate for new collaborative relationships between schools, state and local governments, and community-based agencies (Crowson and Boyd, in press; Guthrie, Scott, Guthrie, and Aronson, 1994; Melaville, Blank, and Asayesh, 1993). Recent interest in learning more about such projects prompted the U.S. Department of Education and the American Educational Research Association to sponsor an Invitational Working Conference on Comprehensive School-Linked Services for Children and Families, held in September 1994 (U.S. Department of Education, 1995).

After over a quarter century in which SI initiatives have grown and evolved, what do we know about those experiences? The literature is surprisingly meager. Even a call by the editors of this volume at the 1994 AEA conference for copies of evaluation reports of SI projects was fruitless.

Knapp (1995) presents a concise literature review of studies of comprehensive, collaborative services. He concludes that although a number of studies of SI projects have been conducted, they tend to be embedded in broader writings about social policy and program development. Published research and evaluation of such projects has consisted primarily of case descriptions and single-project assessments; discussions of the special methodological issues associated with SI projects are just now beginning to emerge.

It is the methodological issues—and their practical implications—that this volume is attempting to address. The remainder of this chapter presents a conceptual framework for defining and describing what human services integration as an intervention is. Knowing more detail about the nature and structure of the "black box" will assist evaluators in establishing linkages between programs or program features (in other words, social intervention theories) and desired goals or outcomes, and in attributing causality between services integration treatments and results. Doing so will enable us to improve program policy and practice.

The following two sections identify the dimensions of SI initiatives and describe those dimensions as functions of the level and intensity of the integration effort. A matrix depicting those categories and possible relationships between the two is presented in Table 1.1.

Levels of Integration

The word *integration* is commonly used as both a catch-all term and a representation of an ideal state, but it may be more accurate to say that it represents a point on a continuum of the various levels and types of interrelationships in any SI initiative (Crowson and Boyd, in press). Although different authors may use different labels for the points on the scale of that continuum, or present them in a different order, the intensity of the level of integration can be characterized as ranging from very loosely structured (the information sharing and communication level) to very unified (the integration level).

In addition, a concept associated with the level of intensity is the degree of formality or informality that governs integrative activities. The degree of formality of those relationships parallels but does not always mirror precisely the level of integration. At their most informal, activities are less likely to be guided by established agreements, protocols, or procedures, and are likely to occur infrequently or on an as-needed basis. The most formal relationships are governed by officially sanctioned, comprehensive written agreements or documents that clearly specify rules and boundaries. The following subsections describe the levels of integration and their degree of formality in more detail.

Information Sharing and Communication. One step above what Heintz has characterized as independent operations (that is, when service systems operate autonomously in a parallel fashion) (Martin, Chackerian,

Table 1.1. Matrix of Services Integration Dimensions and Levels of Integration

Intensity of Integration Continuum

Dimensions	Information Sharing and Communication	Cooperation and Coordination	Collaboration	Consolidation	Integration
	← *Informal*			*Formal* →	
Partners					
Target population					
Goals					
Program policy and legislation					
Governance and authority					
Service delivery system model					
Stakeholders					
Planning and budgeting					
Financing					
Outcomes and accountability					
Licensing and contracting					
Information systems and data management					

Imershein, and Frumkin, 1983), the information sharing and communication level represents a very informal relationship in which entities share general information about programs, services, and clients. Communication may or may not occur on a regular basis and may differ depending on the functions and authority levels of the staff involved. Examples include sharing of informational brochures, educational presentations, newsletters, videotapes, and joint staff meetings.

Cooperation and Coordination. The cooperation and coordination level is still largely informal, representing a loosely organized attempt by autonomous agencies and programs to work together to change procedures or structures to make all affected programs more successful (Vandegrift and Sandler, 1993). Examples include reciprocal client referral and follow-up processes between agencies and programs, verbal agreements to conduct joint staffings, mutual agreements to provide priority responses, or joint lobbying for legislative change or funding requests.

Collaboration. The collaboration level is usually formalized, but could still operate informally (at least for a brief period). Activities at this level are shared; still-autonomous agencies and programs work together as a whole with a common goal, product, or outcome. Partners are equal (Vandegrift and Sandler, 1993; Guthrie, Scott, Guthrie, and Aronson, 1994). Examples include partnerships with written agreements, goals, formalized operational procedures and possibly joint funding, staff cross-training, or shared information systems.

Consolidation. A consolidated system is often represented as an umbrella organization with single leadership in which certain functions (usually administrative) are centralized, but line authority is retained by categorical divisions (Martin, Chackerian, Imershein, and Frumkin, 1993). In many activities there is a high degree of cross-program collaboration, coordination, cooperation, or information-sharing. Examples include government agencies with responsibility for numerous human services programs.

Integration. A fully integrated activity or system has a single authority, is comprehensive in scope, operates collectively, addresses client needs in an individualized fashion, and is multipurpose and cross-cutting. Categorical lines are transparent, activities are fully blended, and funding is pooled. Eligibility requirements for all services are simple and uniform. Clients' problems are treated as a whole and individuals are treated as part of family and community systems. Examples might be one-stop shops in which unified intake and assessment, case management, and many services are provided in one location, and one entity has sole responsibility for management and operational decisions.

Dimensions of Human Services Integration Initiatives

In surveying the myriad SI projects that have been developed in recent years, the various models and approaches that have been designed, and the general literature on SI initiatives, it is clear that any such initiative has a number of dimensions on which the level of integration may vary in its nature and intensity (Martin, Chackerian, Imershein, and Frumkin, 1983; Kahn and Kamerman, 1992; Children's Action Alliance, 1994). Different authors highlight certain dimensions over others, group them differently, or include only certain dimensions in their discussions of SI (Kusserow, 1991b). However, certain key dimensions are common to most SI initiatives and are described in the next sections.

Partners. Who are the major organizations involved? Under whose auspices is the project operating? In which sectors does each operate? What are their individual sources of authority and their interrelationships?

Any two or more agencies or organizations in any combination may be involved in or sponsor a services integration initiative. Placement of this dimension on the integration continuum applies to their interrelationships outside of the SI project. In other words, to what extent are they integrated before forming the partnership? For example, each partner may be completely independent or autonomous, such as a school, county social service agency, and private corporation. Some partnerships might be independent, whereas others may consist of two or more programs or agencies administered by a single government department (for example, a school district in collaboration with a state agency that provides child welfare and public assistance offices on campus). A partnership could consist solely of two or more programs within a single administrative agency (for example, a city or county multipurpose service center).

The level of integration might apply horizontally: a group of programs within similar service domains, regardless of administrative entity, might join together; it might also apply vertically, to the extent that various levels of government, the community, and the private sector within appropriate program areas join together (Cohen and Ooms, 1993).

The general categories of organizations commonly found in SI partnerships include government (including specific programs, agencies, or departments), private nonprofit, private for-profit (such as service providers and hospitals), schools, universities, charitable foundations, commercial businesses and corporations, and public policy research organizations (such as the Urban Institute and the Heritage Foundation).

Target Population. Toward whom are the programs and services directed? Who are the intended users? Who is the project expected to affect?

SI projects differ in the types of populations they serve, from very narrowly prescribed to very broadly defined (for example, pregnant Hispanic teens who have dropped out of school, or all people with incomes below the poverty level). It is most difficult to apply the concept of the integration continuum to the target population. The continuum could be translated in this instance to mean the range of specificity or breadth of inclusion of population groups with certain characteristics. In that case, the widest possible integration category would be anyone in the general population in need of a service (as with general information and referral hotlines).

Another key aspect of services integration might be substituted in the discussion of this dimension. Regardless of the particular characteristics of the target population involved, how does the project view the population, and at what level are its services directed (individual, family, extended family, peer group, neighborhood, community, and so on)? The higher levels of integration would occur at the neighborhood and community levels (as long as they also include services for specific individuals). For example, a neighborhood resource center might provide assessment and case management for families. A child in a family receiving case management may need a recreational program as a deterrent to gang activity, and the center may provide a late-night supervised baseball or basketball program on-site, in which that child could participate, that would also be open to the neighborhood.

Goals. What is the SI initiative expected to accomplish? To what extent are the initiative's goals consistent with the goals of individual partners?

The level of goal integration for an SI project is the extent to which there is a shared vision, philosophy, or set of guiding principles that reflect and are agreed on by the partnership as a whole. A project may have both a set of global, overarching goals and specific subgoals for each partner or program.

Program Policy and Legislation. What categorical programs are included in the initiative and what is their statutory basis? What are the specific features and provisions of each program? What services are provided? How extensive are any regulations?

Services integration projects consist of any number of programs and services, many of which are prescribed independently (with only occasional references to cross-program coordination) in legislation and implementing regulations (Wingspread Conference, 1993). The composition of programs and the particular service mix in an SI project depend on the target population and the specific needs to be addressed (for example, parenting skills, life skills, family planning, and secondary or basic education for teen parent dropouts; or job search, skills training, work experience, and supportive services for unemployed public assistance recipients).

Because the self-contained, categorical nature of most programs represents a major deficiency of the human services system—a deficiency SI initiatives are designed to address—the level of integration for this dimension is the extent to which program policies (such as eligibility requirements, service specifications, terms of financing, and quality assurance) are unified and reflected formally in statutes, administrative rules, and policy manuals.

Governance and Authority for the Services Integration Initiative. Who is responsible for the SI initiative? Who makes final decisions and how are they made?

Although partners in an SI initiative are likely to retain their autonomy and independence as organizations, the project itself must establish some guidelines and procedures for decision making. Even if an authority structure is not established overtly, a de facto structure will certainly emerge.

At informal levels of integration, consensus among all partners may be sufficient for decision making. More formalized arrangements include intergovernmental agreements or memoranda of understanding. One agency may be designated by an elected executive or legislative body to take the lead among a group of participating organizations.

In a briefing paper prepared for the May 1993 Wingspread Conference on "Going to Scale with a Comprehensive Services Strategy," Morrill reviewed several types of governance structures that have been used or attempted for SI initiatives:

Elected officials from general or special-purpose governments form a governing panel with self-selected or rotating leadership.

A steering committee composed of agency leaders, community leaders, and elected officials is designated by statute or executive order and reports to a body of elected officials.

A special-purpose authority may be created by statute with revenue-raising capabilities, overseen by a board whose representatives are appointed by sponsoring government jurisdictions.

Metropolitan councils of governments that have established memberships and rules of decision making may be used.

These are only a few of many possible governance models, each with its own advantages, disadvantages, and level of effectiveness.

Service Delivery System or Model. How are the goals of the SI initiative carried out? How are service delivery structures and relationships designed and organized, both functionally and geographically?

The service delivery system or model is the largest dimension of an SI project and has numerous subcomponents, each of which varies on the integration continuum. Some of the key components and the bases for determining their level of integration are as follows:

Communications. At the staff service delivery level, the extent of formal written communications, policy and procedures manuals, newsletters, staff meetings, forums, and so on within the SI project.

Staff deployment and reporting. The extent to which the project is administered as a unified venture, and lines of authority and reporting are linked to project management versus a categorical program or home agency management; the extent to which staff are generalists versus providing program-specific functions.

Training. The extent to which staff are trained across the programs participating in the project, and the extent to which the project is presented to them as a unified venture.

Geographic location and service configuration. The extent to which project services are provided in one location and how they are configured. Examples include autonomous programs located in the same building; single-program case management in one location with referrals to off-site programs; a case manager in one location leading a team of case workers from off-site programs; common intake and assessment in one location, with referral to a lead case manager based on primary need, and further referrals to other sources on- or off-site; teams of front-line workers who are based at one site and have program-specific expertise, co-located workspaces, and shared caseloads; one person providing case management at one location for all programs in the project, with most or all services provided on-site; and an individual outreach worker who takes unified case management functions out to families in their homes and communities.

Case management. The extent to which program-related case management is provided by one person, an interdisciplinary team of people, or by independent (program-specific) case managers; the scope of the case manager's responsibilities (such as assessment, referral, purchase of services, monitoring, and follow-up).

Other. Other subdimensions of the services delivery system or model include the extent to which eligibility requirements and determinations remain categorical or are unified, and who conducts them; the extent to which all needs and problems of the presenting client and his or her family are assessed; and the extent to which referral and follow-up procedures are unified, formalized, and comprehensive.

Stakeholders. How are stakeholders considered and involved in the project? Are all constituencies represented? Are service recipients included in project planning, operations, and oversight?

The level of integration for this dimension is likely to be measured by the extent to which stakeholders for all organizational partners and for all target populations of the project are identified and addressed collectively, and the extent to which the project is presented to them in a unified manner (Guthrie, Scott, Guthrie, and Aronson, 1994).

Planning and Budgeting. How are needs determined? How are resources requested, allocated, and deployed?

The level of integration includes the extent to which service needs and levels are determined jointly, using common needs assessments and including relevant stakeholders in the process. Also, depending in part on how funding sources are structured, the extent to which project budget development is coordinated or conducted jointly is a measure of the level of integration on this dimension (Wingspread Conference, 1993).

Financing. What types and sources of funding are available? How can they be combined? What restrictions exist and how are expenditures accounted for?

Most current services integration projects involve partners with separate and distinct funding sources. Clearly, a key measure of a project's level of integration is the approach to and extent to which those resources are combined to support the initiative (Wingspread Conference, 1993; Ooms, 1991).

In the proceedings of the 1993 Wingspread Conference on "Going to Scale," Frank Farrow outlines various financing strategies that reflect the different levels of integration. Those strategies are adapted below for this discussion:

Retaining existing categorical funding streams, but delegating authority over those streams from the partners to the project's policy-making and administrative authorities.

Redeploying existing dollars from ongoing program operations to the joint venture, or from higher-cost to lower-cost services, and using the savings for the SI project.

Leveraging private sector and foundation dollars to pay for startup costs or to expand the SI project funding base.

Refinancing federal entitlements to allow a broader (multiprogram) funding base.

Pooling existing dollars across program and agency lines into a common, unified fund from which to administer the SI initiative.

Investing, reinvesting, or creating new grants or appropriations that will fully fund the SI project.

Another measure of integration for this dimension is the extent to which financial accounting is unified or conducted jointly, uses the same standards and procedures, and so forth.

Outcomes and Accountability. How does the SI initiative define success? How are performance measures determined and how broadly do they apply? What types and levels of outcomes are selected? How are they measured, tracked, and used?

The extent to which outcomes represent the overall goals of the services integration initiative, encompass the key levels of impact (in other words, individual, family, service delivery system, and community levels), and address both the programmatic and partnership aspects of the initiative are ways to assess the level of integration. A major accountability (and evaluation) question may be the extent to which a certain degree of integration in a project is cost-beneficial, as opposed merely to whether the project achieves a greater or lesser level of integration (on any one or all dimensions) or whether it is more effective and efficient than reverting to the traditional model of providing services on an individual program basis.

Licensing and Contracting. How are providers and services procured? How are materials and products obtained? How are standards set and quality assured?

A measure of the degree of integration in this area is the extent to which partners are able to unify provider licensing and contracting functions, such as the adoption of common terminology, standards, and contract types, and centralized or unitary certification, quality assurance, or procurement procedures (Children's Action Alliance, 1994).

Information Systems and Data Management. How are automated data systems structured and used to support the SI initiative? How are data recorded and shared? What provisions are made for confidentiality and what restrictions apply?

Possibly the truest measure of the extent to which an SI initiative is integrated is the degree to which automated information systems for client eligibility, service use, tracking, payments, and outcomes are developed or linked (Cohen and Ooms, 1993). Although a single data system that encompasses all partners and participating programs would be the most unified, the majority of SI projects are likely to be formulated by partners with entirely separate information collection mechanisms and capabilities. Some partners may have highly sophisticated, well-established, self-contained automated data systems; for others, data collection may be minimal and automation support virtually nonexistent. Short of starting from scratch to create a customized system, some examples of the levels to which systems integration might be achieved include system interfaces that allow cross-file updating, ability to link records and conduct cross-program data matches, creation of a shared interagency data base with program-specific subsystems that support multiple applications, and production of joint, project-level reports.

Other measures of the level of information systems integration include the extent to which computerized information on project participants and activities is made available at the individual, family, and program levels to all levels of staff; confidentiality requirements are mutually accommodated; and informed consent and data-sharing agreements are in place.

Each of the above dimensions can vary along the continuum of integration, as can the degree of formality or informality. The degree of formality is likely to be most blurred in the middle ranges of the continuum. A final point about the dimensions of SI projects is that this catalogue is not exhaustive, and other dimensions not mentioned here may certainly be identified and developed by evaluators, depending on their specific projects.

Evaluation Issues and Questions

Ideally, having a framework for identifying and defining what is in the "black box" of a services integration intervention will assist evaluators in developing appropriate methodologies and interpreting results. But that is only the beginning of the issues and questions facing evaluators of these complex and multidimensional projects. Some fundamental questions include the following:

What aspects of the initiative should be measured? There appear to be three levels of interest: the effectiveness of individual components (individual- and family-level outcomes), the integrating effects of the partnership process and the new service delivery model as it is applied to individual program and service components (the new service system effects), and the combined effects of the program and system components (synergistic effects).

What tools exist or are needed for measuring the levels of integration?

To what extent are outcomes due to the strength and effectiveness of each categorical program, regardless of the SI effort? Conversely, to what extent are outcomes due to the integrative aspects of the SI project alone, regardless of the effectiveness of any individual program or service component? How are program effects disentangled from the integration model and from its several dimensions (each with varying levels of integration)? This could be an important point if one program is known to be particularly successful on its own. Do the results reflect the fact that the one program is carrying the model, or is there truly value added by the combination?

Is it legitimate to use program outcomes to assess SI projects that may not be directly related to the collaboration itself (in other words, for which there may not be a strong causal linkage) (Labin, 1994)? Should program-specific indicators be avoided as measures of successful integration?

What is the relative importance or contribution of each of the SI dimensions, which can vary independently as well as together?

To the extent that conclusions can be drawn about the effectiveness of the SI initiative and its contribution to the outcomes, are such partnerships worth the time, money, effort, and political capital? Are different combinations of levels of integration on any particular dimension more cost-effective than others? What are the trade-offs?

Is it possible that a project might contain the wrong combination of programs or services, which could contribute to ambiguous or negative results (in other words, the partnership is well-integrated, each program or service is implemented appropriately and has been proven individually to be effective, but a key component may be missing so the integration effort appears to be successful, even though there are no effective client outcomes)?

Is a totally integrated project an ideal project (in other words, a standard against which to measure achievement)? Perhaps an additional approach to evaluating the partnership and integration aspects of the initiative is to develop an ideal model of an integrated services structure for a particular project and evaluate against that? Conversely, is total integration on every dimension necessarily appropriate, and does it really achieve the optimal configuration?

Evaluation practitioners will be grappling with these and other issues, and developing creative solutions to them as the SI movement approaches the twenty-first century.

References

Bruner, C. "Going to Scale: Challenges in Service Design" (briefing paper). Wingspread Conference, "Going to Scale with a Comprehensive Services Strategy," summary notes. Columbia University, National Center for Service Integration, 1993.

Children's Action Alliance. *The Partnership for Children: A Re-Design of the System for Arizona's Children and Families*. Phoenix: Arizona Community and Tucson Community Foundations, 1994.

Cohen, E., and Ooms, T. *Data Integration and Evaluation: Essential Components of Family-Centered Systems Reform*. Washington, D.C.: American Association for Marriage and Family Therapy Research and Education Foundation, 1993.

Crowson, R. L., and Boyd, W. L. "Structures and Strategies: Toward an Understanding of Alternative Models for Coordinated Children's Services." In J. G. Cibulka (ed.), *Coordination Among Schools, Families and Communities: Prospects for Educational Reform.* Albany: SUNY Press, in press.

Farrow, F. "Going to Scale: The Importance of Financing" (briefing paper). Wingspread Conference, "Going to Scale with a Comprehensive Services Strategy," summary notes. Columbia University, National Center for Service Integration, 1993.

Guthrie, L. F., Scott, B. L., Guthrie, G. P., and Aronson, J. Z. *Portraits of Interagency Collaboration.* San Francisco: Far West Laboratory for Educational Research and Development, 1994.

Kagan, S. L. *Integrating Services for Children and Families: Understanding the Past to Shape the Future.* New Haven, Conn.: Yale University Press, 1993.

Kagan, S. L., Goffin, S. G., Golub, S. A., and Pritchard, E. *Toward Systemic Reform: Service Integration for Young Children and Their Families.* Falls Church, Va.: National Center for Service Integration, 1995.

Kahn, A. J., and Kamerman, S. B. *Integrating Services Integration: An Overview of Initiatives, Issues, and Possibilities.* Columbia University, National Center for Children in Poverty, 1992.

Knapp, M. S. "How Shall We Study Comprehensive, Collaborative Services for Children and Families?" *Educational Researcher,* 1995, *24* (4), 5–16.

Kusserow, R. P. *Services Integration: A Twenty-Year Retrospective.* Washington, D.C.: U.S. Department of Health and Human Services, Office of the Inspector General, 1991a.

Kusserow, R. P. *Services Integration for Families and Children in Crisis.* Washington, D.C.: U.S. Department of Health and Human Services, Office of the Inspector General, 1991b.

Labin, S. M. "Collaborative Services Analysis." Unpublished paper, 1994.

Martin, P. Y., Chackerian, R., Imershein, A. W., and Frumkin, M. L. "The Concept of 'Integrated' Services Reconsidered." *Social Science Quarterly,* 1983, *64* (4), 747–763.

Melaville, A. I., Blank, J., and Asayesh, G. *Together We Can: A Guide for Crafting a Profamily System of Education and Human Services.* Washington, D.C.: U.S. Department of Education, 1993.

Morrill, W. "Forms of Governance 'At Scale'—Questions, Precedents, and Alternatives" (briefing paper). Wingspread Conference, "Going to Scale with a Comprehensive Services Strategy," summary notes. Columbia University, National Center for Service Integration, 1993.

Ooms, T. *Coordination, Collaboration, Integration: Strategies for Serving Families More Effectively, Part II: State and Local Initiatives.* Washington, D.C.: American Association for Marriage and Family Therapy Research and Education Foundation, 1991.

U.S. Department of Education and American Educational Research Association. *School-Linked Comprehensive Services for Children and Families: What We Know and What We Need to Know.* Washington, D.C.: U.S. Department of Education and American Educational Research Association, 1995.

Vandegrift, J. A., and Sandler, L. "Evaluating Business Partnership Programs in Education: What Defines a Successful Venture" (briefing paper). Morrison Institute for Public Policy, School of Public Affairs, Arizona State University, Phoenix, 1993.

Weiss, H., and Halpern, R. *Community-Based Family Support and Education Programs: Something Old or Something New?* Columbia University, National Center for Children in Poverty, 1990.

Wingspread Conference. *Going to Scale with a Comprehensive Services Strategy,* summary notes. Columbia University, National Center for Service Integration, 1993.

ELLEN L. KONRAD is manager of the Office of Evaluation in the Arizona Department of Economic Security.

This chapter explores the conceptualization and design of studies that evaluate integrated services initiatives and suggests approaches for further evaluation of how these initiatives work and what they are accomplishing.

Methodological Issues in Evaluating Integrated Services Initiatives

Michael S. Knapp

The explosion in attempts to integrate human services has brought a new set of challenges for evaluators. Voices calling for integrated services initiatives as a solution to the needs of so-called high-risk families and children have built to a crescendo across the past decade and especially the last half dozen years. In the process, this category of social intervention has captured the attention of policy makers, advocates, and the public. Claims, advocacy, and advice about integrated services initiatives are proliferating, as are pilot experiments. All at once there is a need to do careful, probing evaluation to sort among the claims and characterize what the experiments have demonstrated.

These social interventions pose special problems for evaluators. This chapter explores these problems by first reviewing methodological issues that confront the evaluator, and then discussing ways to approach these issues. Several remarks about the nature of the problems and my assumptions about evaluation introduce the discussion.

What makes integrated services initiatives difficult to evaluate is their complexity and flexibility, the nature of collaborative or integrated effort, and the convergence of different disciplines. Evaluation designs must first accommodate the sheer number of players, stakeholders, and levels of the system, as services join forces to influence the lives of families and children. Evaluation design stretches further to handle the flexible tailoring of effort that is frequently part of integrated services. Furthermore, as discussed in Chapter One, the extent to which programmatic efforts are integrated defies easy conceptualization, no less

This chapter is adapted from "How Shall We Study Comprehensive, Collaborative Services for Children and Families?" *Educational Researcher,* 1995, 24 (4), 5–16. Copyright 1995 by the American Educational Research Association. Adapted by permission of the publisher.

description or assessment. Finally, the act of studying such endeavors engages evaluators from traditions that do not normally communicate with one another.

A few further comments will explain assumptions about evaluation that underlie this chapter. Drawing on work by authors such as Scriven (1974), Cronbach and Associates (1980), and Patton (1978), I consider evaluation to include any systematic attempt to inform broad stakeholder audiences and policy communities about the implementation or effects of social interventions, not just investigations of whether initially stated program goals are achieved and to what degree (such designs typically pay too little attention to goal evolution and unanticipated implementation matters over time). In addition, I make no clear distinction between formative and summative evaluation purposes, or process versus impact studies. In short, I assume that all evaluations are essentially formative (Cronbach and Associates, 1980) and that proper attributions of impact to cause require one to understand the processes that produced the impacts (Patton, 1978).

Issues Confronting Evaluation of Integrated Service Initiatives

Three sets of issues—related to diversity of perspectives, independent and dependent variables, and attribution of effects to causes—confront evaluators wishing to make sense of integrated services initiatives. These issues are present in studying many complex interventions, but they are demonstrably acute in this case. The issues have been framed using conventional causal terms—independent and dependent variables—not to imply that a particular evaluation paradigm is most appropriate, but rather to use a language widely understood by members of the evaluation community.

Engaging Diverse Perspectives. Integrated services initiatives—and attempts to study them—inevitably involve the perspectives of multiple stakeholders, participants, and professional disciplines. For example, if a given initiative combines public health nursing with social work, substance abuse counseling, and health science teaching, the perspectives of those professional disciplines are inescapably involved. In addition, it would be hard to examine the initiative without considering the perspectives of agency leaders and policy-making or sponsoring groups. Finally, more than professional perspectives are involved. The ways clients or consumers of services construe their needs, perceive attempts to help them, or think about appropriate interventions are relevant to understanding what is going on and even to framing questions and evaluation designs.

How should all these perspectives be represented in the design, conduct, and interpretation of evaluation? There is no easy answer, and the answer always reflects the political context of asking and answering questions about a particular initiative. Multidisciplinary evaluation teams can help represent different professional traditions, though finding a common working language is not a trivial task. It is harder still to bridge the language gap between the evaluators and program recipients. Some evaluators try closing this gap by engaging the recipients as collaborators in the evaluation process (Weiss and Greene, 1992). As in any area of evaluation, studies of integrated services initiatives carried out in the public eye implicate powerful stakeholders who are involved in the initiative under study, have an interest in its outcomes, or sponsor the evaluation. The diversity of such stakeholders may reduce the evaluator's room to maneuver, necessitating compromises that may gain an audience's support while weakening the study's evidence base or design logic.

Capturing Independent and Dependent Variables. The issues here are in part a matter of conceptualization and in part a matter of measurement. Of the two, I will argue that the former poses the more pressing issues: at the root of many measurement problems is the task of constructing and operationalizing theories of social needs and intervention.

Specifying the Independent Variable. Consider, first, the integrated services themselves. Like other broad domains of social reform (for example, school restructuring), the integration of human services takes many forms. This makes for an independent variable—the programmatic factors presumed to bring about results for individuals or systems—of some complexity. In many integrated services initiatives, the independent variable itself ceases to be a fixed treatment, as conventionally assumed by experimental evaluation designs, and becomes instead a menu of possibilities and supports that facilitate consumers' interaction with these possibilities.

Integrated services initiatives range from relatively low-intensity efforts meant to coordinate the work of different professionals to intensive, highly integrated arrangements (the framework in Chapter One reviews a range of intervention types that fall somewhere on the continuum of possibilities). In addition, such initiatives often take place on multiple levels of the human service system and may target changes in the actual services available to families and children (Philliber Research Associates, 1994), the service-providing system (White, 1993), or both (Wehlage, Smith, and Lipman, 1992). Thus, services for individual children or families often presume some form of integration at higher levels, among individuals and organizations providing management support to direct service providers—school principals, clinic directors, field supervisors—or at the policy-making level, among school districts, state social service agencies, and so on.

The fact that so many kinds of arrangements share the same generic label cries out for ways to conceptualize the differences in terms of common dimensions, and there have been numerous attempts to do so (Crowson and Boyd, 1993; Kagan, 1991; Schorr and Both, 1991; Golden, 1991; Morrill, Reisner, Chimerine, and Marks, 1991). At a minimum, the following dimensions are involved. First, as noted above, integrated services initiatives may address system reform primarily, actual services provided to families and children, or both. Second, the arrangements differ in the extent to which services are actually changed or redefined through integrative effort, or simply relocated or made more accessible. Third, the degree to which resources, control, and power are shared among the collaborating partners varies. Fourth, the scale and scope of arrangements vary enormously, from local arrangements involving only two service sectors to statewide initiatives joining many sectors (see Chapters Four and Five, this volume). Finally, arrangements differ in what might be termed the flexibility or mutability of treatment—that is, the degree to which services provided to any child or family are individually tailored or changeable over time. This feature is especially problematic: if each consumer accesses the human service system in a different way, or in a way that changes over time, then there may be no clear programmatic independent variable to study (Kagan, 1991).

Because the independent variable has many meanings, both across and within integrated services arrangements, evaluators may often be talking past each other, and not about the same thing, even within the same study. Regardless of the conception of integrated services employed, the intervention generally comprises multiple, often separate components. Simply multiplying the number of independent variables (as in multivariate correlational designs) is no real answer; one rapidly runs out of analytic capacity to handle and interpret the many discrete variables that come to mind, and one misses the glue that may bind these elements together into a more integrated whole. The evaluator is left with difficult questions: How to describe the independent variable(s) under study? What are its conceptual boundaries? What is not part of the independent variable(s)? What are the most meaningful units (and levels) of analysis? What indicators most efficiently capture the presence and mutability of the independent variable(s)?

Delimiting the Dependent Variables. As varied as the independent variables may be in studies of integrated services initiatives, so may the dependent variables be. Whatever the stated goals of integrated services arrangements, the evaluator's attempts to pinpoint outcomes must accommodate the large number of possible outcomes, their interdependence, and the range from discrete, modest outcomes to those that are more global and complex. Consider the following child and youth outcomes, offered as a core list on which to base accountability (adapted from Schorr, 1994): healthy births (indicated by decreases in low-birth-weight babies and births to school-age mothers, and increases in utilization of prenatal care), immunization (for example, the rate by age two), readiness for school (indicated by remediation of preventable health problems, no signs of abuse or neglect, and so on), successful school participation (indicated by high achievement in school and low rates of truancy or suspensions), avoidance of problematic behaviors (for example, school-age pregnancy and substance abuse), self-sufficiency among young adults, and adequate family income (for example, levels over the poverty line).

The wide range of possible outcomes is compounded when an initiative encourages different arrangements across sites, or when services are individualized for each consumer; in such cases, evaluators must attend to many kinds of outcomes, although not necessarily for whole populations. Furthermore, if the outcomes represent a developmental progression over time, as in the list above, then later outcomes are dependent on earlier ones, and the ultimate impact of the integrated services will have to be tracked over long periods.

The outcomes described above apply to individuals and groups, and despite some difficulties in measurement, are relatively discrete and clear. System outcomes are generally less discrete or clear than those applying to individuals. Take, for example, the challenges in capturing system outcomes such as the community embeddedness of service systems (Bruner, 1994), the shared authority implied by integrated forms of service organization and funding (General Accounting Office, 1992), or deep-structure systems changes (Crowson and Boyd, 1994). The more human service systems are organized and operate in fully collaborative and integrative ways, the more complex and elusive the outcomes become. For example, while it is relatively easy to measure change in referral rates or use of co-located services, it is much harder to capture beliefs about integrated practice that might evolve as the co-located professionals interact.

So the evaluator confronts fundamental questions of ends for which the integration of services is the means. What ends (including, but not limited to, stated program goals) might result from the integration of services? How many outcomes can be meaningfully considered and at what level (individual, program, system)? What outcomes conceptually represent steps taken toward more ultimate ends? What is not an outcome of the initiative in question?

Attributing Effects to Causes. The complexity and mutability of the independent variable, combined with the large number of and interrelationship among dependent variables, generate an attribution task of the first magnitude. To what do we attribute the level of dependent variables noted above, for children and families who participate in integrated forms of human service?

The director of a study evaluating a statewide integrated services initiative described the problem this way:

> If we measure benefits for kids and families, what do we say contributed to it? Their individual services? The "program" as it existed in the three months they were involved? . . . The program in one month is not the same as the next (a new partner joins the collaborative, changing the mix of staff, the number of services, the level of trust or conflict in the collaborative, and so on). . . . There is so much going on out there, so much flux that even if we can document change or improvement, we have little idea what to attribute it to. We have one school in the study that is an integrated early childhood program site, site of a Blue Cross managed-care experiment, a new charter school, the recipient of a state restructuring grant, and in a neighborhood that is the recipient of family preservation funds. If we measure improvement in health indicators for the children, is it the early childhood program or the managed-care experiment? If there are educational benefits, is it the peer tutoring in the early childhood program or the restructuring grant or the "charter school-ness"? [M. Wagner, personal communication, July, 1994]

Evaluators who study complex social interventions are used to this problem in one sense: they commonly acknowledge that most outcomes worth studying are multiply caused. But the number and elusiveness of the relevant independent variables make this situation especially challenging. Add to the attribution task the difficulty of explaining why certain children fail at school or why disenfranchised families experience multiple problems with which they are unable to cope (see Dym, 1988, regarding ecological views of the family; Knapp and Woolverton, 1995, regarding the role of social class in schooling). Pervasive social conditions place individuals and groups in a disenfranchised position; human services have only a limited capacity to address questions of social position.

Ways to Address the Issues

Resolving the three sets of issues in particular instances is too dependent on context, and there are too many such instances for a short chapter such as this to offer specific advice about evaluation questions or study designs. But it is possible to characterize more globally attributes of evaluation that accommodate the matters just raised and to suggest approaches likely to yield useful insights into the operation and effects of initiatives.

Desirable Attributes for Evaluation of Integrated Service Initiatives. To be helpful in making sense of integrated services, evaluation studies need to be strongly conceptualized, descriptive, comparative, constructively skeptical, positioned from the bottom up, and collaborative (when appropriate).

Strongly Conceptualized. Carefully constructed conceptual frameworks can clarify what is being studied and illuminate assumptions on which programmatic initiatives rest. At a minimum, evaluators need to make explicit the conceptual dimensions underlying the initiatives under study; many ways of identifying dimensions are possible, and some promising ones have been suggested (see, for example, the references noted in discussing the independent variable). Two further kinds of conceptual models operate within a given integrated services initiative, and it is up to the evaluator to make them explicit, and hence open to inspection.

First, integrated services initiatives rest on assumptions about the people whom these services are intended to serve and the conditions that generate their need for service. Programs operating on a deficit model, for example, tend to locate the problem in the "high-risk" child or family. There are good reasons to view such models as insufficient and unhelpful. More successful conceptualizations of the problem may consider the joint roles played by social conditions, individual circumstances, and institutional expectations or routines (Dym, 1988; Richardson, Casanova, Placier, and Guilfoyle, 1991).

Second, the program's "theory of action" (Patton, 1978; Chen, 1990; Weiss, 1995) presumes links between programmatic effort and the problem at hand. To take a simple example: consider an integrative services arrangement that co-locates a health worker and social worker in high schools to provide advice and counsel to youth who are likely to become pregnant, spread sexually transmitted diseases, or engage in other destructive behaviors. The arrangement assumes that the presence of these individuals will increase access to good advice and, when needed, treatment; in addition, the presence of these professionals in the school, it is assumed, will stimulate referrals from teachers and others. By spelling out this strategy, evaluators (and participants) have the chance to examine the logic of intervention. Is it reasonable to presume that presence will increase access? Are there other mediating factors that influence whether the presumed relationship would hold? Ultimately, data can be gathered to test the assumptions on which this logic rests.

Some provocative and helpful conceptual work has begun to appear in the literature. Treatments of the phenomena within overarching ecological frameworks (Dym, 1988; Mawhinney, 1993) provide compelling accounts of how child development, family welfare, and family service interventions operate in community and institutional contexts. Discussions of professional and institutional norms (Mitchell and Scott, 1993) provide further theoretical grounds for understanding what supposedly collaborative professionals do. This work complements attempts to examine services integration in terms of the "deep structure" of norms, rules, routines, and administrative scripts within service-providing institutions (Crowson and Boyd, 1994).

Descriptive. If services integration can be so many different things, then it makes sense to emphasize the description of particular cases of integrated services initiatives. Ideally, such descriptions should be guided by (and should inform) the strong conceptual frameworks called for above; endless narrative and detail will not serve any useful purpose. Qualitative "thick" descriptions, though not the only kind of useful account, are especially helpful in illuminating what integrated arrangements mean to participants, how such efforts differ from service-as-usual, and what the nature of integration is. Careful descriptions are needed of at least the following: organizational arrangements; the interface between the consumer and the collaborating service providers; the sharing of resources, ideas, and professional work; the experience of integration; and the extent and nature of change in the consumer's behavior, attitudes, or life circumstances.

Comparative. Given strong conceptualization (which permits cross-case comparison) and good description, the stage is set for meaningful comparative studies that seek to maximize what can be learned from the natural laboratory of initiatives currently under way. Such studies are unlikely to offer the kind of comparisons inherent in experimental or quasi-experimental studies, but they can illuminate the range of conditions that support or frustrate integrated programs, as well as possible forms of promising practice. Whenever contrasting cases can be chosen to vary on key conceptual dimensions, studies can offer powerful comparative insights.

Constructively Skeptical. Evaluation needs to help audiences see through hype, prescription, and program rhetoric while remaining sympathetic with program goals (and sensitive to the politics of reporting evaluation findings). Skepticism is called for regarding many claims made on behalf of integrated services initiatives, among them assertions regarding cost savings, mutually reinforcing effects, attribution to programmatic efforts, stability of integrated arrangements, incentives for integration, and changes in approach to service.

Keeping a skeptical stance constructive in evaluative situations is obviously complicated. Program opponents are likely to use negative evidence as ammunition in debates about program continuation, while program promoters may wax defensive at the hint of criticism. In addition, the unrealistically high expectations and short attention span of most policy communities makes skepticism problematic. But there is no great virtue in prolonging the lifetime of interventions that rest on shaky logic and little evidence. The trick is to preempt or resist pressures to apply evaluation questions, designs, or measures inappropriately to the program in question by prematurely searching for impacts at a relatively early stage in program development, for example.

Positioned from the Bottom Up. Services are ultimately integrated as they converge on individuals, groups, or target populations. Evaluations that trace backward from the experiences, behavior, perceptions, and status of service consumers will be more likely to show if and how the integration occurred and whether it achieved valuable ends. Such studies focus on the consumer and the consumption of services, but need not be solely concerned with the consumer's-eye view of integrated services initiatives. For example, in sketching its evaluation strategy for the New Futures initiative, the Annie E. Casey Foundation envisioned three components, one of which would feature individual profiles of youth undergoing change, another assembling data related to aggregate impact on youth, and the third examining institutional effects (Center for the Study of Social Policy, 1987). Such designs prominently feature the nature and meaning of service and system benefits at the ground level, while offering evidence for such benefits in specific local settings.

Collaborative. Because it is essential to engage diverse perspectives in studies of integrated services initiatives, it is tempting to expect evaluation itself to be collaboratively designed and implemented, either by evaluators from different disciplines or by evaluators and participants (service providers, consumers) in the programs under study. Discussions that emphasize a partnership between evaluators and program staff contribute to the call for more collaborative evaluation of integrated services (Weiss and Greene, 1992). There are obvious advantages to putting heads together in such a way: drawing attention to conceptual elements that one evaluation tradition might ignore, identifying the assumptions and perspectives of different professions, developing more appropriate measures, and finding multiple meanings in results. Dialogue with service consumers regarding evaluation goals, approaches, or findings can probably help evaluators stay tuned to consumers' perspectives (easily forgotten as professionals focus on serving or helping clients). However, these advantages should not obscure what we know about the difficulty of collaborative practice (Golden, 1991)—lessons that are no less applicable to evaluation than to service delivery. Good collaboration is difficult and time-consuming (a challenge to evaluations, which typically must be done on tight budgets), requires a sharing of control (while the logic of many study designs calls for tight control), and may risk co-opting the evaluator as shared perspectives and interpretations are developed.

Some Promising Evaluation Approaches. Realizing these attributes calls for studies that combine different traditions of evaluation. Without minimizing differences in assumptions, I argue that different traditions—for example, those supporting qualitative and quantitative inquiry—are both necessary and complementary in making good sense of integrated services initiatives for the many audiences who wish to understand these social interventions.

Six examples follow of evaluative studies or study components that embody the attributes discussed above and are likely to yield useful insight at this stage in the understanding of integrated services. None of these six approaches constitutes a comprehensive investigation analogous to most of the major evaluations now under way; however, these kinds of studies can be viewed as components of a large investigation.

Profiles of Individual Participation and Change. This kind of study answers the questions, How does the individual child or family participate in integrated services? What does participation involve? In what ways do these individual participants change? By treating the individual's participation and experience as the primary unit of analysis, investigations of this sort bypass the problem of treating the whole program as a meaningful or fixed treatment. Qualitative and quantitative data can both be part of the profile. Sampling of individuals to study (and gaining access to these individuals) becomes a major issue; depending on the size and complexity of the sample, such investigations could present a picture of integrated services initiatives across the range of people within a community, or even multiple communities.

Multiple-Case, Thick Descriptions of Integrated Services at the Point of Service Delivery. This sort of study represents a kind of programmatic counterpart to the preceding one. Rather than focusing on the consumer, it examines the nature of professional work and the contexts in which this happens, and answers the questions, What do professionals do to integrate their efforts at the point of service delivery? What forces and conditions influence their attempts to address social needs? The rationale for this kind of study presumes that integrated service involves subtle shifts in professionals' conceptions of their craft, work routines, and approach to particular consumers; qualitative approaches are especially suitable for capturing such phenomena. This kind of evaluation is needed to characterize, both conceptually and empirically, the elusive independent variable in integrated services arrangements. Comparative attempts to describe and contrast different kinds of integrated arrangements, chosen to vary along key dimensions, would be particularly helpful.

Quantitative and Qualitative Analyses of the Costs of Integrated Service Initiatives. The costs of integrated services arrangements are likely to be both high and hard to interpret; audiences need to know whether the costs of these services are simply prohibitive for all but a few children and families. The deceptively simple questions to answer are, What do integrated services initiatives cost the human service system, the public, and the consumer? Are these costs worth it, in terms of definable benefits or effects? Because most such initiatives are experimental, start-up costs need to be disentangled from ongoing costs. Furthermore, various kinds of costs must be considered, including time, energy, complexity, and burden on service providers or consumers. Ultimately, forgone opportunities for less labor-intensive ways of addressing human needs and long-range failure to address the needs of children and families must also be factored into cost analyses. Costs need to be examined comparatively, with full-service arrangements contrasted with less comprehensive ones. Though difficult to obtain, reliable numbers are important to pursue, as are attempts to characterize qualitatively the nature of cost. To date, there is little work that examines such costs responsibly, though some have argued the importance of doing so (White, 1988).

Single-Subject (and Single-System) Time-Series Evaluation to Demonstrate Impact on Individuals or Service Systems. It is essential to answer the bottom-line question, What do integrated services initiatives do for children, families, and human services systems? But getting at this matter through group comparative designs, the most common approach to ascertaining impact, may be fruitless when interventions are so individualized, meaningful control groups hard to construct, and attribution of result to cause complicated to trace. In such instances, the individual unit's behavior over time may well be its own best control, as argued by the tradition of single-subject time-series evaluation. Such designs call for baselines of repeated measures over time prior to participation in integrated services, a fully described treatment, and follow-up repeated measures demonstrating change in trajectory associated with exposure to treatment. Though complicated to apply to many integrated services initiatives in their conventional form (for example, as practiced in special education evaluation), time-series designs can be adapted to the purposes of studying such initiatives. An analogous design logic pertains at the organizational level to get at the impacts of system reforms (Knapp, 1979).

Investigations of Exemplary and Typical Practice. In this kind of study, the evaluator works backward from instances of presumably effective or average practice to explanations for the apparent success. This study answers the questions, What do apparently successful integrated services initiatives accomplish and how do they accomplish it? What forces and conditions enable these services to do what they do? Presuming that through some combination of reputation and outcome indicators one can identify instances of integrated services initiatives that seem to do good things for children and families, careful study of these instances using both qualitative and quantitative means (but ideally with some kind of quantitative outcome indicators) should be especially instructive. By including sites that represent typical practices, the evaluator can cast the accomplishments of exemplary sites (and the conditions that support these accomplishments) in perspective.

Analyses of Data from Management Information Systems. A sixth kind of analysis also has promise although it faces significant obstacles in practice. Evaluators and program designers alike have noted the importance, as well as the difficulty, of getting succinct data that track how people interact with services, especially where these services are separately housed and governed by restrictions on the flow of information.

Experiments have been undertaken to create information systems that record presumably comprehensive provision of service (see Family Impact Seminar, 1993, for a summary of related work). In theory, such tools may be useful for answering questions such as, What services have families X, Y, and Z used, and when? What did service providers do in attempting to meet the needs of children A, B, and C and their families? What changes in indicators are associated with which patterns of service use? Such systems are only as good as the data put into them, however, and it is not easy to ensure that high-quality data are entered and regularly updated. Often, more data are collected than necessary for evaluators' or any user's purposes; this can quickly feel burdensome to participants at the street-level, especially if data collection is imposed from the top down. Their efforts to gather high-quality data are greatest when systems provide them with information they want and can use; when such information corresponds with what evaluators need to know and where their access to such information is politically and organizationally feasible, this device has considerable potential.

When Evaluation Approaches Are Unlikely to Yield Useful Results. At the current stage of understanding of integrated services initiatives, not all approaches to evaluation are likely to yield useful results, or do so in all the situations confronting evaluators. Meta-analytic studies, for example, are likely to be premature, given the lack of a commonly defined independent variable or comparable outcomes among the studies that have begun to merge (although there are some useful integrative reviews such as Schorr and Both, 1991). Factor-analytic studies, which attempt to address the multiplicity of forces by correlating hundreds of variables, risk identifying statistical clusters that are impossible to name meaningfully. Even group-comparative experimental studies may be inappropriate in many instances, despite their wide popularity among evaluators and their audiences, and persistent arguments that such designs offer the most rigorous and useful knowledge about the effects of complex social interventions (Rossi, 1992; Gomby and Larson, 1992). Let me elaborate on this last point, to illustrate the potential problem.

The obvious advantages of group-comparative designs include the compelling logic and apparent rigor of experimental contrasts (where the assumptions on which this logic rests hold) and the familiarity and credibility of this form of knowledge generation among many audiences. But the drawbacks are many, as some have suggested (Bruner, 1994; Family Impact Seminar, 1993; Weiss and Greene, 1992). The challenge is to ensure that key assumptions are viable (for example, Is there an identifiable and uniform treatment? Are recipients and nonrecipients sufficiently comparable?). As has been learned from years of social experiments, including studies of programs that are much more easily specified and applied to groups (for example, job training programs), group comparative studies are harder to realize in practice than on paper, and the logic often breaks down. A great danger exists that the requirements of the evaluation design will force evaluable situations to be constructed that compromise or limit what integrated services initiatives are attempting to do. A similar danger is that the press for experimental results will force a premature search for evidence of widespread impact—just the thing that new and ambitious programs are least able to provide, regardless of their merits.

Call for Appropriate Evaluation of Integrated Service Initiatives

In conclusion, this chapter urges evaluators, and those who sponsor or demand studies, to consider what is appropriate to ask and answer at the current stage of development, experimentation, and understanding. Integrated services initiatives are generally not mature programs that have developed a relatively stable modus operandi; in most cases we are witness to rapidly evolving experimentation within turbulent reform contexts. The class of intervention is hard to name and describe. In this context, it is debatable what we should be evaluating.

In such circumstances there are sound reasons to engage in many kinds of evaluation. We may wish to keep the early program rhetoric, filled with visions and promises, from being taken as gospel long before we know whether anyone is helped or whether we can afford it; just as likely, we may wish to keep impatient audiences from losing faith in integrated services because no evidence appears of instant impact. Furthermore, there are a sufficient number and variety of investments in integrated services initiatives to afford numerous opportunities for learning and various forms of natural experiments. And the children and families who are the consumers of integrated services are too needy and too numerous to ignore.

But in our rush to evaluation, there are some big dangers of which to be wary. For one thing, we may end up studying only what we know how to study, and not engage in the methodological learning that new forms of social intervention require. For another, we may prematurely declare the experimentation a failure, neglecting to be clear about what failed. Or, we may proclaim programmatic victory, only to find that multiply served children continue to fail in school while their families confront health and social challenges with which they still cannot cope. Finally, in attempting to join multiple evaluation traditions, we may attract so many evaluators to the phenomenon of integrated services initiatives that service providers and the consumers they are trying to help feel besieged. These are avoidable failures. The evaluation community can and must transcend such traps if it is to help society learn from, and about, this promising form of social intervention.

References

Bruner, C. "A Framework for Measuring the Potential of Comprehensive Services Strategies." In N. Young, S. Gardner, S. Coley, L. Schorr, and C. Bruner (eds.), *Making a Difference: Moving to Outcome-Based Accountability for Comprehensive Service Reforms.* Falls Church, Va.: National Center for Services Integration, 1994.

Center for the Study of Social Policy. *New Futures Evaluation Strategy*. Washington, D.C.: Center for the Study of Social Policy, 1987.

Chen, H-T. *Theory-Driven Evaluation*. Newbury Park, Calif.: Sage, 1990.

Cronbach, L. J., and Associates. *Towards the Reform of Program Evaluation*. San Francisco: Jossey-Bass, 1980.

Crowson, R. L., and Boyd, W. L. "Coordinated Services for Children: Designing Arks for Storms and Seas Unknown." *American Journal of Education*, 1993, *101*, 140–179.

Crowson, R. L., and Boyd, W. L. "Achieving Coordinated, School-Linked Services: Facilitating Utilization of the Emerging Knowledge Base." Paper prepared for the Invitational Conference on Improving Urban Schools: Better Strategies for the Dissemination and Utilization of Knowledge, Arlington, Va., Sept. 1994.

Dym, B. "Ecological Perspectives on Change in Families." In H. B. Weiss and F. H. Jacobs (eds.), *Evaluating Family Programs*. New York: De Gruyter, 1988.

Family Impact Seminar. *Data Integration and Evaluation: Essential Components of Family-Centered Systems Reform—Background Briefing Report*. Washington, D.C.: American Association of Marital and Family Therapy Evaluation and Education Foundation, 1993.

General Accounting Office. *Integrating Human Services*. Washington, D.C.: General Accounting Office, 1992.

Golden, O. "Collaboration as a Means Not an End: Serving Disadvantaged Families and Children." In L. B. Schorr, D. Both, and C. Copple (eds.), *Effective Services for Young Children—Report of a Workshop*. Washington, D.C.: National Academy Press, 1991.

Gomby, D. S., and Larson, C. S. "Evaluation of School-Linked Services." *The Future of Children*, 1992, 2 (1), 68–84.

Kagan, S. L. *United We Stand: Collaboration for Child Care and Early Education Services*. New York: Teachers College Press, 1991.

Knapp, M. S. "Applying Time Series Strategies: An Underutilized Solution." In L-E. Datta and R. Perloff (eds.), *Improving Evaluations*. Newbury Park, Calif.: Sage, 1979.

Knapp, M. S., and Woolverton, S. "Social Class and Schooling." In J. Banks and C. M. Banks (eds.), *Handbook of Research on Multicultural Education*. New York: Macmillan, 1995.

Mawhinney, H. "Discovering Shared Values: Ecological Models to Support Interagency Collaboration." In L. Adler and S. Gardner (eds.), *The Politics of Linking Schools and Social Services*. London: Falmer Press, 1993.

Mitchell, D. E., and Scott, L. D. "Professional and Institutional Perspectives on Interagency Collaboration." In L. Adler and S. Gardner (eds.), *The Politics of Linking Schools and Social Services*. London: Falmer Press, 1993.

Morrill, W. A., Reisner, E. R., Chimerine, C. B., and Marks, E. L. *Collaborations That Integrate Services for Children and Families*. Washington, D.C.: U.S. Department of Education, 1991.

Patton, M. Q. *Utilization-Focused Evaluation*. Newbury Park, Calif.: Sage, 1978.

Philliber Research Associates. *An Evaluation of the Caring Communities Program at Walbridge Elementary School*. Accord, NY: Philliber Research Associates, 1994.

Richardson, V., Casanova, U., Placier, L., and Guilfoyle, K. *Students At-Risk*. London: Falmer Press, 1991.

Rossi, P. "Strategies for Evaluation." *Children and Youth Services Review*, 1992, *14* (1–2), 167–191.

Schorr, L. B. "The Case for Shifting to Outcome-Based Accountability." In N. Young, S. Gardner, S. Coley, L. Schorr, and C. Bruner (eds.), *Making a Difference: Moving to Outcome-Based Accountability for Comprehensive Service Reforms*. Falls Church, Va.: National Center for Service Integration, 1994.

Schorr, L. B., and Both, D. "Attributes of Effective Services for Young Children: A Brief Survey of Current Knowledge and Its Implications for Program and Policy Development." In L. B. Schorr, D. Both, and C. Copple (eds.), *Effective Services for Young Children—Report of a Workshop*. Washington, D.C.: National Academy Press, 1991.

Scriven, M. "Goal-Free Evaluation." In E. House (ed.), *School Evaluation: The Politics and Process*. Berkeley, Calif.: McCutchan, 1974.

Wehlage, G., Smith, G., and Lipman, P. "Restructuring Urban Schools: The New Futures Experience." *American Educational Research Journal,* 1992, 29 (1), 51–93.

Weiss, C. "Nothing as Practical as a Good Theory: Exploring Theory-Based Evaluation for Comprehensive Community Initiatives for Children and Families." In J. P. Connell, A. C. Kubisch, L. B. Schorr, and C. H. Weiss (eds.), *New Approaches to Evaluating Community Initiatives: Concepts, Methods, and Contexts.* Washington, D.C.: Aspen Institute, 1995.

Weiss, H. B., and Greene, J. G. "An Empowerment Partnership for Family Support and Education Programs and Evaluation." *Family Science Review,* 1992, 5 (1–2), 131–148.

White, K. R. "Cost Analyses in Family Support Programs." In H. B. Weiss and F. H. Jacobs (eds.), *Evaluating Family Programs.* New York: De Gruyter, 1988.

White, W. A. "California's State Partnership for School-Linked Services." In L. Adler and S. Gardner (eds.), *The Politics of Linking Schools and Social Services.* London: Falmer Press, 1993.

MICHAEL S. KNAPP *is associate professor of educational leadership and policy studies at the College of Education, University of Washington.*

The federal evaluation of forty-one Community Integrated Service Systems projects is described, focusing on issues in conducting a national, cross-site evaluation and the findings of the implementation study of the first two years of the initiative.

Evaluating the 1992 and 1993 Community Integrated Service Systems Projects

Richard N. Roberts, Barbara H. Wasik

Evaluation at the Federal Level

Provision for evaluation is still an afterthought in a great many federal and state-supported human service programs. Systematic evaluation of federal programs is of recent origin, and was introduced in the programs of the Office of Economic Opportunity. Other federal programs in education and the social services gradually adopted the practice of providing for third-party evaluations, and health programs were perhaps the slowest to fund such independent evaluations. As a result, it is not unusual for evaluators to be called in after a program has been launched, after the grants have been awarded, and often too late to affect the evaluability of a program or even to collect uncontaminated baseline data. Furthermore, because program designs often represent an opportunistic compromise between an agency's interest and congressional mandates, there can be considerable ambiguity as to the goals of the program, its underlying assumptions, and the kind of information to be collected.

The evaluation reported here was funded under three separate contracts from the Maternal and Child Health Bureau, one each to the Early Intervention Research Institute, Utah State University, Logan, and to the School of Education, University of North Carolina at Chapel Hill (UNCH) for the 1992 projects and one to the UNCH for the 1993 projects. The authors gratefully acknowledge the editorial assistance of Jules M. Marquart and Ellen Konrad in the preparation of this manuscript.

All of these issues have been important considerations in the development of the implementation evaluation reported in this chapter for the Community Integrated Service Systems (CISS) projects funded by the Maternal and Child Health Bureau (MCHB) of the Department of Health and Human Services. In this chapter, the background leading to the funding of the forty-one CISS projects is first described, followed by a discussion of the MCHB's interest in an evaluation of the implementation of the projects. Then the framework for the implementation evaluation and selected findings of the study are presented to illustrate the need for such a framework to guide the evaluation process.

An initial review of the individual project proposals and evaluation plans before development of the evaluation framework suggested the diversity of the forty-one community-based efforts and the lack of common objectives and outcome measures. This finding, confirmed in a subsequent and more detailed analysis, required the development of an evaluation framework for describing the implementation of the overall effort. Thus a framework was developed that relied less on individually collected project data and more on data that allowed for cross-site analyses. The chapter concludes with lessons learned from the planning and execution of this evaluation plan relevant to national evaluation efforts.

How CISS Came to Be

Over the past several decades, the MCHB has increasingly strengthened its commitment to the development of integrated services at the community level that are both responsive to the needs of families with very young children and that encourage local solutions to the development of effective systems of care. In its present form, this commitment is seen in efforts to promote family-centered, community-based, coordinated, and culturally competent care (Koop, 1987; Roberts, Wasik, Casto, and Ramey, 1991; Brewer, McPherson, Magrab, and Hutchins, 1989; Wasik, Roberts, and Lam, 1994; Bronheim, Keefe, and Morgan, 1993; View and Amos, 1994).

One of the MCHB's most recent initiatives to promote integrated service systems is the CISS projects. They were planned to help communities develop systems of care designed to reduce infant mortality and to improve health outcomes for mothers and children through an integrated set of services established at the community level. The CISS initiative was developed over the course of several years in response to congressional mandates to reduce infant mortality through home visiting programs and a continuing interest within MCHB to assist communities and states in their efforts to develop more family-centered, community-based, coordinated systems.

Through its block grant program, MCHB has increased technical assistance to states and communities to encourage the development of more effective service systems. The MCHB wants to promote more coordination among agencies and private and public providers, reduce duplication, and enhance resource use. At the same time, Congress has directed MCHB to begin a home visiting program in order to address the high rate of infant mortality in the United States. Thus, the CISS initiative has been responsive to both a very specific congressional mandate tied to a funding source and an MCHB objective to help communities develop the capacity to create efficient systems of care and to improve the outcomes for children and families.

Over a two-year period, two requests for proposals (RFPs) have been published, one to fund thirty-two programs in 1992 and one to fund nine more in 1993. Differences in the two RFPs reflect the evolution of MCHB's policy development with respect to integrated systems and set the stage for the evaluation issues to be described.

1992 and 1993 CISS Objectives

The purpose of the CISS effort, as defined in the 1992 project RFP, was to achieve "a reduction in infant mortality and improved health outcomes for mothers and children . . . through the expansion and development of community integrated service systems." Support for the need for CISS accompanied this proposition, including "the high rate of infant mortality in the U.S., elevated risk factors for pregnant women and mothers of young children, and finally the fragmented and discontinuous and sometimes inaccessible or unavailable nature of services to mothers and very young children." Six strategies were proposed in the 1992 RFP to be used in addressing these problems, including home visiting, one-stop shopping, not-for-profit community-based initiatives, provider participation in publicly funded projects, MCHB projects serving rural populations, and outpatient and community-based program alternatives to inpatient institutional care (Roberts and Wasik, 1994).

The focus of the 1993 CISS projects was broader in scope than the first 1992 funding cycle. It extended the population to include all pregnant women and children and identified a specific set of principles that was to be incorporated by each funded project. The specific purpose of the 1993 CISS initiative was stated as follows: "In order to respond to the needs for coordinated services, MCHB has established the development of community-based service systems as a top priority. The systems are intended to promote physical, psychological, and social well-being for all pregnant women, children, adolescents and their families; provide individual attention to their specific health care needs; and link health care and other services, including early intervention, educational, vocational, and mental health services" (Department of Health and Human Services, 1993, p. 1).

As part of the 1993 CISS guidance, ten principles of an integrated service system were outlined: provision of care should be family-centered, community-based, coordinated, universal, comprehensive, collaborative, culturally competent, developmentally oriented, accessible, and accountable (Wasik, Lam, and Kane, 1994).

MCHB's Interest in Evaluation

As the CISS projects were about to begin, the MCHB was aware that the forty-one individual projects represented a diverse set of community-based solutions to a common problem defined through the RFPs. Because each RFP provided different guidance for program development to potential grantees, the evaluation effort needed to describe the projects funded under each RFP. The evaluation effort described in this chapter was conducted with two goals in mind: to provide a comprehensive, cross-project description of the initial planning and implementation efforts of all forty-one projects and to provide the foundation for a longitudinal study.

A cross-project study was needed to provide information on the scope, diversity and similarities in project demographics, conceptual models underlying program efforts, implementation issues faced by projects, and data collection efforts. Each of the programs emerged from a unique set of community needs and already existing resources. The group or agency that responded to the RFP did so with an understanding of the problems and dynamics within its local community, and its belief in the most appropriate solutions to them. In some cases, efforts had been underway for some time within local agencies to solve the issues raised by CISS. In other cases, the CISS initiative was the stimulus to identify and address the perceived needs in a more systematic and systemic way. The boundaries of the CISS projects themselves were not clearly defined and were but one part of a larger, ongoing systems integration and development effort within each community. Although each project was required to include an evaluation plan that assessed its progress in meeting program goals, a broader analysis of this initiative was needed.

Second, MCHB was interested in a more extensive longitudinal evaluation to clarify the evolution of the CISS projects and to describe the policy context in which they were developed. Such information could be useful in developing policy and providing technical assistance to these projects and to other communities. The evaluation effort described here provided information to MCHB on its first goal of project description and set in place the baseline data for a longitudinal developmental evaluation. Project descriptions of the initial implementation efforts for the 1992 projects can be found in Roberts and Wasik (1994); for the 1993 projects, see Wasik, Lam, and Kane (1994).

In addition to the initial implementation studies described here, the authors have proposed two additional studies that would obtain common information on all projects over time to examine their procedures, policies, and outcomes. The first of those two studies is a longitudinal, nonexperimental descriptive investigation designed to address questions in three areas: conceptualization and design, project implementation, and project outcomes. These three areas are consistent with the evaluation framework proposed by Rossi and Freeman (1993), who identify evaluation research encompassing three related activities: analysis related to the conceptualization and design of interventions, monitoring of program implementation, and assessment of program effectiveness and efficiency. Such a study would make it possible to describe the actual procedures and strategies of the forty-one projects and to compare these with strategies derived from the literature.

The second study is proposed as an intensive policy analysis at each major administrative level, from the U.S. Congress to the local community, to assess policy development, approval, and implementation of the CISS initiative. This analysis would be conducted over time using a combination of qualitative and quantitative methodologies to examine the relationship between policy processes at different administrative levels. Interviews and case record reviews would be conducted to assess the services provided and families' perceptions of services they had obtained. This type of forward and backward mapping strategy has been used in other studies of federal initiatives (for example, Dunst and others, 1991) to determine whether there is consistency across administrative levels with respect to particular principles that guide an initiative and whether families who use these services can detect those differences as intended.

The combination of these two proposed studies would use multiple informants and methodologies to triangulate data to answer a series of questions. In so doing, it would make possible a more rigorous evaluation than can be obtained by using only process and outcome data planned by each of the forty-one projects. In the next section, the general usefulness of the local project evaluation plans in developing the overall framework of the cross-site evaluation is discussed.

Relationship of Individual Project Evaluations to the Cross-Site Implementation Evaluation

Each project was required to develop and implement an individual evaluation plan that documented its progress toward its stated objectives. Over the course of development of the implementation evaluation framework, it became clear that data collected by individual projects to meet their own needs would not be useful in answering questions posed at the cross-site federal level because the domains in which individual project data were collected were idiosyncratic to project goals and not amenable to cross-site data reduction.

Plans for evaluation or program monitoring across the forty-one sites varied widely both in the scope of the proposed evaluations and the measures to be collected. Some projects contracted with local universities or colleges to conduct an external evaluation. Other projects were part of a larger community effort and may have had an extensive evaluation plan from the umbrella agency incorporating the CISS projects. A third option exercised by several projects was to monitor the effects of their program through data collection efforts by their own project staff. When the project was evaluated internally in this manner, the evaluation plan was most likely to be skeletal, with minimal process and outcome measures selected.

Independent of who conducted the evaluation, there was relatively little consistency across programs with respect to the types of measures to be used in the major outcome categories. Consensus was also lacking on which categories would be evaluated. Even so, projects generally had at least one measure for each major outcome category. Almost all projects collected at least one measure of birth outcomes. Measures most often cited included low birth weight and infant mortality. Child health was most commonly measured by the frequency of the use of WIC and immunization rates. Abuse or neglect was rarely proposed as a child health outcome measure. Child developmental outcomes were rarely proposed to be measured by almost all projects, probably because of the costs involved in doing so.

The measure most often proposed for maternal health was the use of prenatal care. Change in life-style behaviors by mothers was rarely proposed as an outcome. Outcome measures for the projects' services ranged from whether parenting education was offered to whether assistance was given in daily living and coping skills. Measures of system change were not proposed by many of the 1992 projects, although three projects did propose a cost-benefit analysis. All projects were faced with a challenge in how to fund a reasonable evaluation plan within the very limited budgets they were awarded.

Examples of Evaluation Plans from Two Projects. Summaries of the evaluation efforts of two of the most complete individual evaluation plans are provided as examples.

Example One. One project was housed in a metropolitan area hospital and used a home visiting strategy to conduct outreach to pregnant minority women in the immediate geographic area who as a group were not using the prenatal, obstetrical, and postnatal follow-up services of the hospital. The project proposal, developed jointly with a local university, included a pilot study, a formative evaluation phase, and outcome evaluation including comparison of program participants' birth outcomes with those of previous hospital patients who gave birth before implementation of the CISS project. Funding for much of this evaluation effort came from sources outside of the MCHB portion of the CISS project. Most of the effort assessed the impact of the project at the client level. This project was similar to many projects in that system-level issues were not a central feature in the evaluation plan. This focus in the projects may be at least in part a function of the focus of the RFPs that emphasized strategies at the client level.

Example Two. This example of an individual project evaluation plan is less ambitious than Example One but is still more ambitious than the majority of the projects. The project contracted with a local research institute at the state university to conduct the evaluation for $20,000. This allocation is higher than found in most of the projects. Results were to be reported to the state Medicaid agency to productively replicate the project elsewhere. The outcome evaluation was to examine three areas: whether the project increased the range of services received by poor pregnant women in the target area, whether birth outcomes improved, and whether child health outcomes were improved during the first year of life. Sources of data for these were to include birth certificates, children's complete medical records, mothers' complete medical records, and surveys of client perceptions. This plan pointed to another common issue faced by projects. In most cases the number of families participating in the project was relatively small due to funding constraints and to the emphasis on providing new services to clients rather than only focusing on system change. The outcome data suggested here required large numbers in the sample to approach stability. For instance, if the infant mortality rate was 15 per 1,000 in a given area, it would be problematic to use infant mortality as an outcome measure for a sample of 200 families. One infant death in such a small sample would make it impossible to draw any conclusions about the impact of the project on this variable.

Both of these examples suggest that within the resources at their disposal, the projects were collecting data to document whether project-specific objectives for clients were reached. From a cross-site comparison perspective, additional questions were of particular importance that could not be addressed by these data. For example, neither project provided a means to evaluate the impact of the project on service integration at the system level to document how agencies in their target communities may have changed basic practices over the course of the project to make services more available. At the client level, objectives were program specific and measures were sufficiently diverse to make aggregating data across sites problematic.

Framework for Implementation Evaluation

In our initial approach to the CISS initiative, we chose a framework that emphasized an analysis of the overall initiative both at the project level and across administrative hierarchies. This framework was driven by the two different goals of MCHB concerning its interest in initial descriptions of the projects and the longitudinal analysis of the development of the CISS initiative described above. To accomplish both of these goals, MCHB would need information that included both a complete description of the programs as they were being developed over the course of time in their local communities (horizontal) and a policy analysis of the overall CISS initiative beginning with the intent of Congress and following its impact down to the local family (vertical). In constructing a list of research questions for the implementation evaluation, the emphasis was on describing how the programs defined the service system and on cataloguing the issues they confronted in implementing their projects.

In order to place a structure on the cross-site descriptive evaluation, a schematic framework for evaluating early intervention programs (Wasik, 1993) was adapted. Figure 3.1 presents a graphic illustration of this framework for conceptualizing the relationship between the major variables in a community integrated system. In this framework, relevant variables could be classified as background, project, and outcome.

On the left-hand side of this figure are listed client and community characteristics hypothesized to shape the delivery model and strategies needed to create an integrated service system. These background variables are hypothesized to influence client and service outcomes. The most basic hypothesis in this framework is that there is a relationship between the background variables and the intervention and between the intervention and the outcomes. Numerous specific relationships can be identified. For example, specific community characteristics can be hypothesized to interact with the project to produce different outcomes.

Figure 3.1. Conceptualization of Relationships for CISS Projects

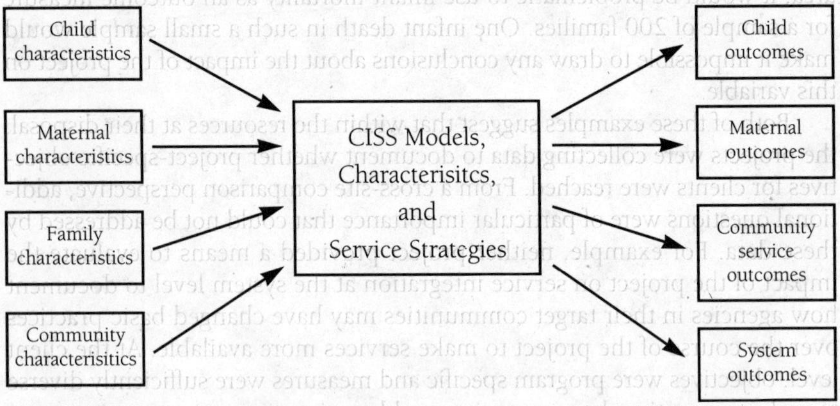

Because each project was idiosyncratic with respect to the background variables listed on the left side of Figure 3.1 and the program components it proposed as the center portion of Figure 3.1, the coding system had to be able to capture the variability within programs while still allowing common features to emerge in data reduction.

The framework described above represents one approach to analyzing the CISS initiatives. In addition to integration at the project level, each project was embedded in an administrative structure that could both support local initiatives and provide direction with respect to program mandates. This larger, ecological context is represented in Figure 3.2. In this framework, the effect is represented as unidirectional for simplicity, although it is understood that a more bidirectional process is at work in most instances.

Cross-Site Implementation Evaluation

In this section, the methods used to conduct the cross-site implementation evaluation are briefly described, summary data with respect to project variation on major variables are presented, and issues in measurement of the variables of interest are discussed.

Methods. As the first phase in the implementation of the longitudinal data collection process, we collected descriptive information on all of the projects within the general framework presented in Figure 3.1 and conducted telephone interviews with the thirty-two projects funded in 1992. We developed extensive forms for recording information from project reports, summary tables, and instruments to assess important variables (Roberts and Wasik, 1994; Wasik, Lam, and Kane, 1994).

Descriptive Cross-Site Results. In drawing conclusions from the CISS projects, the first challenge that faces an evaluator is their extreme variability. Projects vary dramatically along a number of variables such as the population

Figure 3.2. Administrative Levels Associated with CISS Policy Development and Implementation

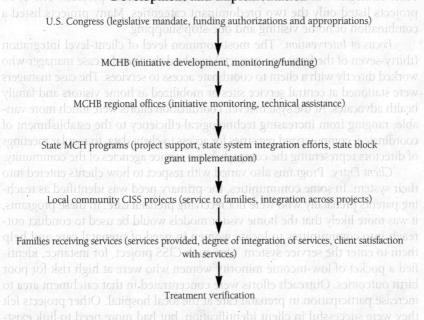

U.S. Congress (legislative mandate, funding authorizations and appropriations)

MCHB (initiative development, monitoring/funding)

MCHB regional offices (initiative monitoring, technical assistance)

State MCH programs (project support, state system integration efforts, state block grant implementation)

Local community CISS projects (service to families, integration across projects)

Families receiving services (services provided, degree of integration of services, client satisfaction with services)

Treatment verification

being served, the geographic location of programs, the strategies being used to create integrated service systems, and the focus of the intervention.

Population. The projects varied widely on the racial and ethnic composition of their target populations. Fourteen projects identified at least 50 percent of their population as European-American. An additional eight projects identified at least 50 percent of their population as African-American, six projects were at least 50 percent Hispanic, and six others were at least 50 percent Asian-American. Native American and Eskimo groups predominated in one or two projects each.

Geography. Of the 1992 and 1993 programs, twenty-three programs characterized their geographic areas as urban or inner-city, fourteen as rural or remote, and six as frontier. Of those programs reporting, the catchment areas ranged from an estimated population of under 25,000 individuals (eleven programs reporting) to a population of over 500,000 (ten programs reporting). Although many programs did not report information on socioeconomic level, over two-thirds of those that did specifically identified a low-income population, and no projects indicated a high socioeconomic status among its target population.

Strategies. Six strategies were outlined in the 1992 CISS guidance and projects were encouraged to use these strategies in developing community integrated service systems. In the 1993 guidance, however, the six strategies were deemphasized and mentioned as options. Projects often used more than one strategy as part of their integrated service system program. Home visiting (thirty-five projects) and one-stop shopping (twenty-nine projects) were the two primary strategies used throughout the forty-one projects. Each of the other strategies was listed by seven or fewer of the 1992 projects. The 1993 projects listed only the two predominant categories. Many projects listed a combination of home visiting and one-stop shopping.

Focus of Intervention. The most common level of client-level integration (thirty-seven of the forty-one projects) involved the use of a case manager who worked directly with a client to coordinate access to services. The case managers were stationed at central service sites or mobilized as home visitors and family health advocates. At the system level, coordination efforts were much more variable, ranging from increasing technological efficiency to the establishment of coordinated, computerized registries for access to client data, to regular meetings of directors representing the comprehensive service agencies of the community.

Client Entry. Programs also varied with respect to how clients entered into their system. In some communities, the primary need was identified as reaching parents prenatally who were not receiving prenatal care. In these programs, it was more likely that the home visitor models would be used to conduct outreach into communities to locate women in need of prenatal care and help them to enter the service system. One such CISS project, for instance, identified a pocket of low-income minority women who were at high risk for poor birth outcomes. Outreach efforts were concentrated in that catchment area to increase participation in prenatal care at the local hospital. Other projects felt they were successful in client identification, but had more need to link existing clients to needed services.

Services Offered. Programs also differed substantially with respect to the services they offered to clients. In some CISS projects, the focus of the intervention was a direct service model in which clients received additional services from the CISS project itself. In other projects, the major focus of the intervention was a referral system that hooked them into other service systems in the community. For example, a number of projects provided direct and referral services to children that included primary pediatric care, WIC, immunizations, disease prevention efforts, and well-baby care. A range of other health services was offered through links with other projects including Healthy Start and dental, hearing, and vision screenings. Child development services were also provided, although usually as referrals for early intervention. A limited number of direct developmental services were provided, such as screening and Head Start Projects (Wasik, Lam, and Kane, 1994).

Results of the Telephone Interviews. The telephone interviews with project directors and staff were important for a number of reasons and illustrate a reactive effect to the evaluation process. Significant portions of the telephone interviews focused on the degree to which projects were actively developing integrated services systems at the system level, due to the lack of such information in most proposals and first-year annual reports. Because most projects focused on service integration at the client level, sensitive project directors picked up the differences immediately in the types of questions that were asked in the phone interview discussions.

In reviewing projects a year later, major shifts had occurred in many of the projects in their efforts to focus more on system level issues. Anecdotal discussions with the project directors revealed that the line of questioning in the interviews helped to refocus their efforts at system level integration. Beyond these iatrogenic effects, much of the data collected from the document reviews could be adequately interpreted only by checking the coded information with the more expansive discussions of project issues over the phone.

System Development Issues. Several chronic issues in service system development emerged as part of this initial descriptive effort. Projects uniformly dramatically underestimated the amount of time it would take to begin the programs presented in their initial proposals. Another issue involved the training of new staff. Many projects felt the need to start serving clients immediately with new home visitors. In doing so, training was given short shrift over the need to hire staff and implement services quickly. An analysis of the content of training suggested a disparity between the initial goal of the community integrated service systems and the training content. Because most programs focused on home visiting models for service provision, home visitors were most often provided training in traditional home visiting topics such as enhancement of child development, prenatal care, how to deliver information, and how to provide family support. Almost no training programs included a strong focus on service integration as the focus of the training itself. Families were not systematically involved in the training effort, although one of the principles of community integrated service systems was family-centered care.

Measurement of Key Process and Outcome Variables. The description of each project's system for integrated services was dependent on measures with appropriate psychometric characteristics that could be used to describe the major variables of interest. In this case, the variables included the six CISS strategies and the ten MCHB principles used to describe integrated services in the 1993 guidance. The variability evidenced across projects suggested that each could be a case study. Yin (1989) described a model of the case study approach that allows a descriptive methodology to be used to summarize across a number of projects with a unifying theme in order to evaluate the utility of the common approach in solving a problem.

In the CISS projects, however, no two projects were identical along any of the dimensions: target population, characteristics of the local community, the services provided, or the outcomes expected to be achieved. This problem was similar to the one faced in the evaluation of the California Healthy Start Initiative described by Wagner and Gomby (this volume). Because there were few constants across the CISS projects, defining variables that could be used in cross-site comparisons became problematic. Each strategy or activity was defined in such different ways within local projects that the term itself did not act as a reliable descriptor of the activities subsumed under it. The variability within any one cluster on how the strategy or activity was operationalized might be as great as the variability between them.

This same process of variable definition is even more problematic for the constructs presented by MCHB as characteristics of a community integrated service system. A community integrated service system is not defined in the first RFP and is defined by the ten principles in the second. Presumably, the degree to which a community integrated services system has been implemented can be measured by the presence of these ten principles. However, the lack of clarity within the RFP and the overall lack of consensus on the necessary components of an integrated service system in the field make definition and measurement of the overall construct difficult (Wasik, Roberts, and Lam, 1994).

In contrast to the ten principles provided by MCHB, Kahn and Kamerman (1993) have developed from the literature a number of common attributes of integrated services systems at the client and system levels. They make it clear that their list is simply the features most reported in the literature and was not empirically derived. Other examples of attempts to define integrated services can be found in Konrad (this volume), Knapp (1995 and this volume), and O'Looney (1994). We know little at this point about the relationship of the items on these lists and the elements that are necessary and sufficient for such a system to operate. Although some attributes have face validity with respect to an integrated system (such as coordination at the client and administrative levels), others such as cultural competence and family-centered care may be orthogonal to the concept. That is, an integrated service system may be insensitive to the need to provide services to clients in a culturally respectful manner and still be an integrated service system. In the same respect, practices within the system may not follow accepted principles of family-centered care. However, the system may be efficient and nonduplicative and have well-articulated case management practices.

Using cultural competence as an example of the need for instrument development, scales for this construct do not exist at the system level, although there have been several attempts to create such instruments (Cross, Bazron, Dennis, and Isaacs, 1989; Roberts, 1990; Roberts and Evans, 1994). Measures with appropriate psychometric properties to be used for program evaluation purposes do not exist at present. However, we have conducted initial pilot work to develop Likert-type rating scales of each of the ten CISS principles (Wasik, Lam, and Kane, 1994). Other examples of evaluation-specific scales to measure service integration and collaboration include the work of O'Looney (1994).

Lessons Learned from the CISS Evaluation

We have learned much over the course of the initial CISS evaluation. Examples of some of the lessons learned continue to reinforce for us the need for consistent external evaluations of federal projects to inform policy and to create feedback loops between programs, evaluation, and policy development that are often lacking (Roberts, 1991; Keough 1990).

Mechanisms at the federal level must be in place to ensure that program evaluation is part of project planning at the conceptual level. In this case, the community integrated service systems were opportunistically funded to serve both a congressional intent and a perceived need within MCHB. Evaluation was approached cautiously and was not seen as necessary to examine the effects of such a policy on system development beyond the individual project level. Because the CISS projects represented one of the first large-scale efforts within MCHB to create more integrated service systems, a well-designed cross-site evaluation plan before project implementation would have helped inform MCHB early in the process with respect to such critical issues as the need for a stronger conceptual framework to guide project development and technical assistance efforts. It would have also pointed to the need to involve all levels of the bureaucratic structure in the conceptualization and implementation of the effort.

Projects being funded as part of a national evaluation or demonstration effort must be held to the standard that ensures that project goals and objectives are stated in ways that can be evaluated. In order for this to occur, the request for proposals must be clear in the questions it asks projects to address. That is, it is not helpful to ask a project to reflect ten principles of an integrated service system when neither the construct of an integrated service system nor the characteristics have been defined. If the goal is to create more family-centered approaches, then specifics regarding the outcomes used to assess the existence of family centeredness must be explicated. Similarly, if objectives that have been tied to increased health indicators for children are included, they should be presented in such a way that data can be obtained (for example, the rate of immunization will increase 10 percent during the first year compared to community local statistics in the preceding year).

A systematic effort to develop measures of the primary constructs associated with community integrated service systems is needed to assist program development and evaluation efforts. The strategy used in this implementation evaluation was to report the most commonly mentioned activities to represent each of the CISS principles and comment on the degree of their convergence. The components of each characteristic identified this way provided for a high degree of face validity, but little in the way of construct or predictive validity. This second phase of validation is crucial to the measures development process and still remains to be done for this set of measures. Measures are not only critical to the evaluation effort, but also needed as a way for projects and policy planners to clearly articulate the goals of the project. From a cross-site perspective, they allow for comparisons that would otherwise be difficult to make.

An evaluation should demonstrate whether programs are meeting an intended target. When a framework is imposed on the evaluative process that assumes a certain logic and connection between background variables, program variables, and outcomes, it should be possible to discern whether those connections exist. Both the initial proposal review and phone interviews with project directors and other key staff clearly indicated that the CISS projects served initially to fill a gap in the service system by providing services to otherwise unserved populations. For some of the programs, however, working to fill the gaps required them to work with other programs. These meetings opened the opportunity for broader discussions with respect to more integrated and unified systems of care.

National evaluations should be driven by the need to evaluate how communities' service systems work together within the ecology of the local community to solve problems for families as well as by how a particular agency's projects have had an impact on the system. As the CISS programs were being developed, several other major service integration efforts were being developed and evaluated at the federal level in other agencies. These included the Part H component of the Individuals with Disabilities Education Act sponsored by the U.S. Department of Education and the Family Support and Preservation Programs developed through the Administration for Children, Youth, and Families. In many respects, all three programs had similar goals in moving toward integrated service systems. Each program was being evaluated independently as part of each agency's need to understand the effect of service integration on their projects.

In some sense, then, we have not moved very far from Secretary Richardson's 1970 comments with respect to the need for more collaboration at each level of service integration from federal agencies to local communities. Other approaches to evaluation that examine community-based efforts to integrate services across agencies have been instructive in this respect. For example, the National Center for Clinical Infant programs (View and Amos, 1994) begins at the community level and describes the ability of agencies to work together with families in creating systems that work for them. Other examples include Communities Can (Bronheim, Keefe, and Morgan, 1993) and the Opening Doors Project (Roberts, 1993). These projects suggest that it is possible to begin such collaborative community-based efforts and to evaluate their impact as they serve families in a more unified, collaborative, and integrative manner.

References

Brewer, E. J., McPherson, M., Magrab, P. R., and Hutchins, V. "Family-Centered, Community-Based, Coordinated Care for Children with Special Health Care Needs." *Pediatrics,* 1989, *83* (6), 1055–1060.

Bronheim, D., Keefe, M. L., and Morgan, C. C. *Communities Can: Building Blocks of a Community-Based System of Care: The Communities Can Campaign Experience* (Vol. 1). Washington, D.C.: Georgetown University Child Development Center, 1993.

Cross, T., Bazron, B., Dennis, K., and Isaacs, M. *Towards a Culturally Competent System of Care: A Monograph on Effective Services for Minority Children Who Are Severely Emotionally Disturbed.* Washington, D.C.: Georgetown University Child Development Center, 1989.

Department of Health and Human Services. *Community Integrated Service System (CISS) Projects, Grant Application Guidance.* Washington D.C.: Department of Health and Human Services, Public Health Service, Health Resources and Services Administration, Maternal and Child Health Bureau, Apr. 1993.

Dunst, C. J., Trivette, C. M., Starnes, A. L., Hamby, D. W., and Gordon, N. J. "Family Support Programs for Persons with Developmental Disabilities: Key Elements, Differential Characteristics and Program Outcomes." *Family Systems Intervention Monograph,* 1991, *3* (1). (Morganton, N.C.: Center for Family Studies, Western Carolina Center.)

Kahn, A. J., and Kamerman, S. B. *Integrating Services Integration: An Overview of Initiatives, Issues, and Possibilities.* New York: National Center for Children in Poverty, 1993.

Keough, B. K. "Narrowing the Gap Between Policy and Practice." *Exceptional Children,* 1990, 57, 186–190.

Knapp, M. S. "How Shall We Study Comprehensive, Collaborative Services for Children and Families?" *Educational Researcher,* 1995, 24 (4), 5–16.

Koop, C. E. *Surgeon General's Report: Children with Special Health Care Needs.* Washington, D.C.: U.S. Government Printing Office, 1987.

O'Looney, J. "Modeling Collaboration and Social Services Integration: A Single State's Experience with Developmental and Non-Developmental Models." *Administration in Social Work,* 1994, 18 (1), 61–86.

Roberts, R. N. *Monograph and Workbook: Developing Culturally Competent Programs for Children with Special Needs.* Early Intervention Research Institute, Developmental Center for Handicapped Persons, Utah State University, Logan. Prepared by Georgetown University Child Development Center, Washington, D.C., 1990.

Roberts, R. N. "Early Intervention in the Home: The Interface of Policy, Programs, and Research." *Infants and Young Children,* 1991, 4 (2), 33–40.

Roberts, R. N. *Best Practices for Home Visiting with Families of Children with Special Health Needs* (#HRSA 93–410[P]). Rockville, Md.: Bureau of Maternal and Child Health and Resources Development, 1993.

Roberts, R. N., and Evans, J. E. "Cultural Competency in Maternal and Child Health Community-Based Programs." In J. C. McQueen (ed.), *Perspectives in Maternal and Child Health.* San Francisco: Jossey-Bass, 1994.

Roberts, R. N., and Wasik, B. H. *The 1992 Community Integrated Service Systems Projects: A Description and Analysis of Initial Implementation Efforts.* Center for Persons with Disabilities, Utah State University, Logan, and the School of Education, University of North Carolina at Chapel Hill, 1994.

Roberts, R. N., Wasik, B. H., Casto, G., and Ramey, C. T. "Family Support in the Home: Programs, Policy, and Social Change." *American Psychologist,* 1991, 46 (2), 131–137.

Rossi, P. H., and Freeman, H. E. *Evaluation: A Systematic Approach.* Newbury Park, Calif.: Sage, 1993.

View, V. A., and Amos, K. J. *Living and Testing the Collaborative Process: A Case Study of Community-Based Services Integration.* Arlington, Va.: Zero to Three/National Center for Clinical Infant Programs, 1994.

Wasik, B. H. *Theoretical Shifts in Early Intervention: Implications for Research and Evaluation.* Chapel Hill: University of North Carolina, 1993.

Wasik, B. H., Lam, K. K., and Kane, H. *The 1993 Community Integrated Service System Projects: A Report of the Initial Plans and Implementation Efforts.* Chapel Hill: University of North Carolina, 1994.

Wasik, B. H., Roberts, R. N., and Lam, W.J.J. *The Myths and Realities of Family-Centered, Community-Based, Coordinated, Culturally Competent Systems of Care.* Proceedings from Scientific Perspectives, Maternal and Child Health Bureau, Bethesda, Md., 1994.

Yin, R. K. *Case Study Research: Design and Methods.* Newbury Park, Calif.: Sage, 1989.

RICHARD N. ROBERTS is professor of psychology, codirector of the Early Intervention Research Institute, and director of research and evaluation at the Center for Persons with Disabilities at Utah State University.

BARBARA H. WASIK is professor of psychology at the University of North Carolina at Chapel Hill, where she is also associate dean for research in the School of Education and a fellow of the Frank Porter Graham Child Development Center.

The policy, political, fiscal, and logistic contexts of California's Healthy Start initiative are described, along with the choices made in accommodating those contexts in the evaluation design and implementation.

Evaluating a Statewide School-Linked Services Initiative: California's Healthy Start

Mary M. Wagner, Deanna S. Gomby

The limited amount of impact data on comprehensive school-linked programs forces policymakers and communities to make decisions about implementing these programs based on process data and intuition. The dearth of short-term impact evaluations of various types of programs coupled with the lack of long-term impact and cost-benefit studies virtually precludes comparisons of school-linked programs with alternative services delivery approaches. . . . Few school-linked programs are planning to conduct the outcome-oriented research that policymakers and program planners need.
—General Accounting Office, 1993, p. 18.

Since that description of the evaluation of school-linked programs was written, more school-linked services initiatives have been launched, and a few more evaluations have been planned. The general description of the state of the field, however, is still true. Very few evaluations of comprehensive school-linked service initiatives exist, partly because of the many political, financial, ethical, and logistic issues that arise when evaluations of such initiatives are planned and implemented. (Recent exceptions include Philliber Research Associates, 1994.) This chapter describes the evaluation of a major statewide initiative, California's Healthy Start, as an example of the balance that evaluators must find between methodological rigor and the realities of evaluating a large public services integration effort.

In this chapter, we define school-linked services initiatives as efforts in which "(a) services are provided to children and their families through a collaboration among schools, health care providers, and social service agencies; (b) the schools are among the central participants in planning and governing the collaborative effort; and (c) the services are provided at, or are coordinated by, personnel located at the school or a site near the school" (Larson and others, 1992, p. 7). Such efforts have been the subject of increasing attention from policy makers and, as of late 1993, at least eight states and hundreds of localities have developed school-linked services initiatives (GAO, 1993). Reviews of these activities by those who hope to inform policy-making also are becoming more common (Larson, 1992; Adler and Gardner, 1994; Dryfoos, 1994).

Proponents of such initiatives contend that part of the reason that some students do poorly in school, behaviorally and academically, is the difficult social and economic circumstances in which they and their families live (for example, pervasive poverty, family dysfunction, and unmet health care needs). Integrated services are advocated as a strategy to help education, health, and social service systems respond to the needs of children and their families in a timely and coordinated way. Schools are a sensible hub for such activities because they are enduring community institutions, they are conveniently located, they already provide a range of educational and noneducational services to children on a universal basis, and they may be perceived as more friendly service sites than many other community institutions.

California's Healthy Start Initiative

In 1991, California governor Pete Wilson signed into law Senate Bill 620, the Healthy Start Support Services for Children Act (Chapter 759, Statutes of 1991). It "authorized the Superintendent of Public Instruction to award annual planning and operational grants to school districts and county offices of education to provide school-based, school-linked integrated health, mental health, social, and other support services for children and their families" (California Department of Education, 1992b). Grantees must demonstrate that they are collaborating with other public and private service providers in developing and implementing their local school-linked services activities.

Coincident with the governor's interest in preventive, school-linked integrated services were the efforts by several private philanthropic foundations within California, which had been independently supporting school-linked services programs throughout the state. Senate Bill 620 offered an opportunity to forge a unique public-private partnership. In 1992, the governor, the superintendent of public instruction, and representatives of the foundations (who had formed the Foundation Consortium for School-Linked Services) signed an agreement in principle to launch the California Partnership for School-Linked Services.

That partnership has three goals: "(1) providing state and local policy, evaluation, and program support for Senate Bill 620 . . ., (2) building a broader statewide comprehensive school-linked service system which cuts across a range of disciplines and agencies, integrating state and local resources to avoid conflicting regulations, fragmentation, duplication, and inconsistent service delivery, and (3) developing mechanisms for refinancing these services through access to Medi-Cal and other funding sources to ensure the availability of health and social services for children and their families in all school districts in the state" (Chynoweth and Henderson, 1992, p. 1).

State general funds are being used to finance the planning and implementation of statewide school-linked services initiatives and related state-level administrative costs. The state budget act of 1993 placed a funding floor under the initiative of about $20 million per year. Additional foundation dollars (about $1.75 million per year) are being used to support an evaluation of Healthy Start and to provide technical support to the California Partnership for School-Linked Services as well as county and local sites as they tackle the issues involved in restructuring service systems for children and families (for example, creating new funding sources and developing county-level capacity for integrating services).

Evaluation is an integral part of the Healthy Start initiative. Healthy Start is essentially an effort to learn what works in providing more comprehensive, integrated school-linked services to children and families; evaluation is the vehicle for that learning. An independent, statewide evaluation was required by Senate Bill 620 and was promised by the partnership in its agreement in principle. In 1992, through a competitive award process, the partnership selected SRI International to evaluate the initiative.

Evaluation Challenges

The SRI evaluation team approached the Healthy Start evaluation with a clear sense of the design, sampling, and measurement characteristics of a rigorous evaluation. Strong evaluations have experimental designs with randomly assigned treatment and comparison groups (either schools, school districts, or children and their families). Ideally, what is being evaluated is clearly defined and controlled across sites so that we understand precisely the intervention creating the outcomes observed. Sample selection criteria are determined by the evaluator and are uniformly implemented at all sites; the sample size is appropriate for the desired level of precision and the anticipated size of impact. Outcomes are multidimensional and uniformly defined and observed across sites. Data are collected by third parties to ensure objectivity of measurement.

The characteristics that make Healthy Start such an exciting initiative, however, are precisely the aspects of the initiative that preclude virtually all of the aspects of rigorous evaluation noted above. The history and goals of the partnership, its multiple funding sources and multiple operational sites, the diversity of those sites in terms of population and program, and the reluctance of some sites to participate in the evaluation have all challenged the evaluators in determining an alternative evaluation approach that maximizes the validity of information produced within the limitations of the initiative's context (see Roberts and Wasik, this volume). The realities of the initiative and their implications for the evaluation approach are described here (see White, 1994, for another discussion of the political and legislative background and context of Healthy Start).

Systemic Change. Healthy Start was launched with the belief that "the development of literate, healthy, productive young adults requires restructuring the way that schools, service agencies and government currently provide services" (Chynoweth and Henderson, 1992, p. 1). The partners in the initiative want funds to be used to create fundamental change in the way services for children and families are delivered. Thus, the initiative does not intend to support programs that give themselves easily to program evaluation (see Konrad, this volume). It intends to sponsor multiple local battles in a broader, statewide revolution in service delivery. The partnership wants to enlist local sites that are ready and willing to fight these battles, and the legislation specifies a competitive grant process as the method for allocating funds to the most capable volunteers. Furthermore, the anticipated service delivery changes are intended eventually to blanket the entire state, with new grants being awarded to new collaboratives each year and with state-level changes applying to all localities. In 1995, after four grant award cycles, 149 operational grants of $400,000 each have been awarded to local collaboratives, as have 280 $50,000 planning grants. Operational grants involve 469 schools in 43 counties, whereas planning grants involve 767 schools in 44 counties.

The funding partners decided that it was not sensible, given their intention to change service delivery statewide, to use a randomized trial design in which some schools, school districts, or collaboratives would be randomly assigned to receive Healthy Start funds while others would be assigned to a control group. A randomized trial design would have frozen both participating and nonparticipating school districts in place for the duration of the trial— a condition that clearly would have slowed efforts at systemic change to an unacceptable degree.

At the individual site level, too, a Healthy Start grant is intended to fundamentally change the ways in which schools function in serving the needs of children and families. All teachers and staff at a site were expected to change how they worked with children and families, not just a select few who might have been serving a small treatment group. Thus, random assignment of children and families within a Healthy Start site also was infeasible.

Multiple Related Policy Initiatives. Healthy Start is not the only recent integrated services initiative in California. At least three other policy salvos have been fired in the battle to change the ways in which services are delivered to California's children and families. The Presley-Brown Interagency Children's Services Act of 1989 (Senate Bill 997), for example, authorizes countywide interagency children and youth services councils that can apply for waivers of state regulations to restructure child and family services. In the same year, the California Department of Education launched Healthy Kids, Healthy California to promote school–community collaboration in designing comprehensive child health programs. Senate Bill 1274 authorizes grants to schools for restructuring school governance and instruction to improve student performance. Some Healthy Start sites have activities operating simultaneously under all these initiatives. If systems change and outcomes improve at the sites, to which policy change should the improvements be attributed? Healthy Start cannot be clearly distinguished from the broader constellation of interrelated policy efforts.

Natural Variation in Interventions. Reflecting the poorly developed state of the knowledge base concerning effective models of school-linked services, the partnership wanted Healthy Start to encourage the widest possible variability in approach so that the relative merits of alternative models could be assessed. Thus, few restraints have been put on local sites in proposing their approaches. The partnership requires only that parents, teachers, students, the school, district and county leadership, and community and agency service providers all be involved in the planning and implementation of Healthy Start (California Department of Education, 1992a) and that local programs link at least four kinds of services at or through the schools, without specifying which services. Beyond these minimal criteria, grantees are awarded points for the extent to which their proposals reflect "an innovative approach to integrated service delivery that is tailored to the specific characteristics of students and family members at the school site" (California Department of Education, 1992a, p. 27).

This approach has succeeded in encouraging wide variation. Sites vary enormously in the goals they have selected for their initiatives (such as improving educational performance, increasing mental health services, and increasing employment) and in the services made available to meet those goals. Programs also vary in the ways in which they have implemented their services (such as school-site family resource centers, satellite service centers, family service coordination teams, and youth service programs). They vary in the number and type of collaborating organizations per site; for example, about two-thirds of the sites link with the county department of mental health or the police or justice system. These differences in participating agencies mean that families are served by staff from a variety of backgrounds, including health, education, social work, and mental health, which undoubtedly flavors the services that families or students receive. Designing a grant-awarding process to elicit variability rather than conformity in approach challenges the evaluation to accommodate sixty-five different programs within a single initiative.

Differences in Populations. The proposed approaches reflect the extreme diversity of California's communities. Sites vary enormously in the populations of children and families they serve. The initiative requires that 90 percent of grant funds be awarded to schools in which at least half of the students are from families that receive Aid to Families with Dependent Children, that have limited English proficiency, or that are eligible to receive free or reduced-price meals. These criteria have not limited the participants a great deal. Participating schools include elementary, middle, and high schools; clients include students and family members that range in age from infancy to adulthood. Ethnic variations are enormous, with some sites having a school population that is predominantly Southeast Asian, for example, and others with populations that are largely Latino. Thus, by design, the initiative confounds the effects of population with program and site.

Individual Experiences of Interventions. A major principle of Healthy Start is that services linked to schools should be family-focused; they are intended to reflect the strengths and goals of individual families and to be delivered to those families in culturally competent ways. One family may be involved with Healthy Start in their school because of the academic difficulties of their third-grader, who comes to school tired because his mother and her partner argue loudly at night and make sleep difficult for the six people who share their three rooms. Another family in the same school may be involved with the same Healthy Start program because of their first-grader's behavior problems that reflect both an unidentified and untreated hearing problem that is isolating the child from his surroundings, and because of the family stress of substance abuse by an older sibling. These two families will experience Healthy Start in very different ways, receiving different combinations of services intended to meet distinct family needs and taking advantage of varying family strengths.

The one intended uniformity for multiply served families is that they have a case manager or family advocate in the program. Case management is required in each Healthy Start site, which includes assessing an individual's or family's needs; developing a case plan for the evaluation, treatment, and care of the individual or family; coordinating the delivery of needed services; ensuring that services are obtained; and monitoring progress to ensure that services are having an impact on the problem (California Department of Education, 1992a). By design, then, the intervention for each participant at a Healthy Start site is intended to be different. Thus, sixty-five intervention models are being manifested in thousands of different experiences of the intervention by individual clients.

Multiple Stakeholders and Expectations. In this complex initiative, stakeholders at the state, county, and local levels all posed different questions regarding the initiative—questions the evaluation is expected to answer. They range from questions concerning the effects of the entire initiative to those involving effects at specific sites. The range includes effects pertaining to systems change and those pertaining to outcomes for schools and for individual children and their families. The range of outcomes also is broad, and includes outcomes relating to health, mental health, and educational performance for individuals and to school completion, violence, and climate. The evaluation reflects these multiple stakeholders and questions. It assesses whether Healthy Start is associated with the development of effective collaboratives, improved service delivery, improved student and family outcomes in multiple domains, and improved school-level outcomes, as they all develop over time. It also attempts to document how improved outcomes, if they occur, are related to the system or service changes that might have been made. The evaluation was also faced with meeting the requirement of Senate Bill 620 to report on early outcomes and their relationship to services by June 1, 1994, only midway through the three-year grant cycle of the first set of operational grantees.

Broad Scope, Limited Funds. The broad range of questions noted above is to be answered in late 1995, as the questions apply to sixty-five sites that have either two or three years of experience with their Healthy Start operational grants. A total of approximately $2.25 million in foundation funds has been allocated for evaluation purposes for three years. Although this is a large amount, it translates into only about $13,250 per site per year—less than many program evaluations that operate at single sites. Fiscal constraints limited the evaluators' range of options, particularly regarding data collection approaches. For example, the very scale of the initiative and the available funds precluded the possibility that the evaluators could collect data directly from the thousands of families that would be served by Healthy Start over three years. Further, the protected relationship between local program staff and their clients made many sites reluctant to permit direct contact between families and evaluators, even if funds had been available to implement that strategy. Thus, program staff have had to supply data to the evaluation regarding both the services provided and the changes in status of the children and families served.

Evaluation Experience of Sites. Participating sites varied in their previous experience with evaluation, their expectations of the Healthy Start evaluation process, and their willingness to engage in it. Although the state requires participation in the evaluation as a condition for receiving grant funds, not all sites were equally willing to supply the evaluators with data. For example, of the forty sites that received grants for operations in 1992, two programs had not submitted any follow-up data at all by early 1995. Sites also varied in the speed with which they were able to implement their programs and, therefore, in how quickly they had any data to report to the evaluation. Some sites were both willing and ready to participate in the Healthy Start evaluation, but were substantially burdened by the sometimes competing demands of multiple evaluations. One site, for example, had nine distinct funding sources for school reform and school-linked services activities, each of which had its own evaluation and data requirements. Local program staff are forced to compromise in meeting the demands of evaluation and the demands of their real jobs: serving clients.

Healthy Start Evaluation Approach

So what is the shape of an evaluation formed in this context of hoped-for systemic change in multiple communities, with multiple stakeholders and goals, that is intended to implement alternative service delivery models to meet the needs of diverse individual families? We describe the choices made by the Healthy Start evaluation team and its partners as it sought to respond to this complex context with the strongest feasible evaluation. We offer this experience not because ideal solutions were found to all challenges faced, but because the experience may be instructive to others who undoubtedly face some of the same complexities in other school-linked services evaluations.

Ongoing Collaboration. Because much is unknown about both implementing and evaluating an initiative of this scope, and because many stakeholders are invested in the outcomes demonstrated by the evaluation, an ongoing process of collaboration was established between the evaluation team, the partnership, and representatives of counties and local sites. Monthly meetings of an Evaluation Working Group during the evaluation's first two years were forums to express concerns about the evaluation that emerged at any level (mostly from individual sites attempting to comply with evaluation data expectations). The meetings also helped to shape the evaluation as decisions were made regarding data collection, analysis, and reporting; to reflect on and to help interpret findings of the evaluation as they emerged; and to decide on midcourse corrections suggested by those findings. The evaluators also have been asked to address groups of stakeholders at various points throughout the evaluation to inform decisions about the integrated services revolution more broadly.

Conceptual Framework. The conceptual framework developed for the evaluation is purposely broad so as to encompass the multiple levels of the initiative and its diversity of stakeholders and evaluation questions. Figure 4.1 illustrates the conceptual framework of the statewide Healthy Start evaluation.

As an innovative state initiative, Healthy Start has generated new relationships and ways of doing business at the state level (Box B) that are to be documented in the process component of the evaluation. Process analyses also are being performed regarding the local collaboratives as they evolve over time (Box C). Their collaborative strategies are intended to result in different approaches to service delivery or models of operation at local sites (Box D). These different models are expected to provide services that are comprehensive, integrated, family-focused, and preventive (Box E). Services will vary in nature, intensity, duration, and other features, depending on the programs providing them and the families receiving them. These new experiences of services are expected to result in improved child and family outcomes for individuals receiving them (Box F) and to aggregate to improved school-level outcomes at affiliated schools (Box G). All of these processes and interrelationships operate within the great diversity of schools, communities, and families that characterize Healthy Start (Box A).

Evaluation Design. As noted earlier, the fundamental goals of the Healthy Start initiative preclude an experimental design to determine its impacts. Thus, the evaluation was designed not to test a single intervention, but rather to help develop knowledge about the implementation and outcomes of alternative interventions that come under the rubric of school-linked services. Therefore, the evaluation involves comparisons among different modes of school-linked services (for example, different kinds and levels of service and different service delivery models) rather than between school-linked services as a single intervention and a no-treatment control group. A repeated-measures design calls for assessing child and family outcomes through comparison of baseline status on multiple measures (such as school performance, use of preventive health care, and self-reported emotional wellness) with the same measures taken at six-month

Figure 4.1. Conceptual Framework of the Healthy Start Initiative

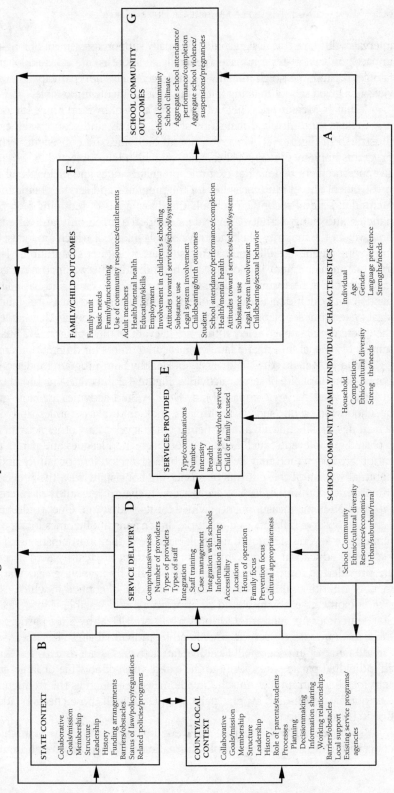

B

STATE CONTEXT

Collaborative
  Goals/mission
  Membership
  Structure
  Leadership
  History
  Funding arrangements
  Barriers/obstacles
Status of law/policy/regulations
Related policies/programs

C

COUNTY/LOCAL CONTEXT

Collaborative
  Goals/mission
  Membership
  Structure
  Leadership
  History
  Role of parents/students
  Processes
    Planning
    Decisionmaking
    Information sharing
    Working relationships
  Barriers/obstacles
Local support
Existing service programs/ agencies

D

SERVICE DELIVERY

Comprehensiveness
  Number of providers
  Types of providers
  Types of staff
Integration
  Staff training
  Case management
  Integration with schools
  Information sharing
Accessibility
  Location
  Hours of operation
  Family focus
  Prevention focus
  Cultural appropriateness

E

SERVICES PROVIDED

Type/combinations
Number
Intensity
Breadth
Clients served/not served
Child or family focused

F

FAMILY/CHILD OUTCOMES

Family unit
  Basic needs
  Family/functioning
  Use of community resources/entitlements
Adult members
  Health/mental health
  Education/skills
  Employment
  Involvement in children's schooling
  Attitudes toward services/school/system
  Substance use
  Legal system involvement
  Childbearing/birth outcomes
Student
  School attendance/performance/completion
  Health/mental health
  Attitudes toward services/school/system
  Substance use
  Legal system involvement
  Childbearing/sexual behavior

G

SCHOOL COMMUNITY OUTCOMES

School community
School climate
Aggregate school attendance/ performance/completion
Aggregate school violence/ suspensions/pregnancies

A

SCHOOL COMMUNITY/FAMILY/INDIVIDUAL CHARACTERISTICS

School Community
Ethnic/cultural diversity
Resources/economics
Urban/suburban/rural

Household
Composition
Ethnic/cultural diversity
Streng ths/needs

Individual
Age
Gender
Language preference
Strengths/needs

intervals. Although this design could potentially support assessment of long-term impacts, only short-term impacts (generally six months) are assessed for many families because their high mobility results in generally short participation in services in a given school, making follow-up measurements impossible.

What Is Measured. The multiple goals of Healthy Start argue for assessing impacts on multiple dimensions of child, family, and school wellness, as illustrated in Figure 4.1. However, not all outcomes are consistent with the programs implemented at all sites, many of which have objected to the extensive measurement battery. For example, pregnancy rates and incidence of gang involvement are relevant measures for the programs and services being implemented at several secondary schools that have goals of reducing teen pregnancies and gang activity. They are considered irrelevant and offensive, however, at the majority of elementary schools, many of which are focused on improving parenting skills and parents' support of children's educations. Therefore, the measurement framework has been divided between core measures (such as school performance, access to primary health care, and basic family needs), for which data are to be collected at all sites, and measures (such as legal system involvement and pregnancy status and outcomes) that are left to the discretion of sites to select if they are relevant to their programs. Thus, the sample of sites, children, and families measured differs for different outcomes.

Who Is Measured. The diversity of Healthy Start program models incorporates a multiplicity of service activities. Figure 4.2 illustrates the broad range of service areas they encompass. Many Healthy Start activities are large-group or schoolwide events, such as health fairs, multicultural assemblies, and vision screenings for all children at a particular grade level. Many other activities are repeated group events, such as after-school recreation leagues and parent education groups, which may be attended by a given student or family once or habitually. Both of these forms of service are consistent with the preventive intention of the initiative, but are not conducive to the kinds of intensive, repeated outcome measurement planned for its evaluation. One would hardly expect to observe differences in multiple dimensions of outcomes for an entire family over several six-month intervals because of their participation in a single parent education event. Only about 25 percent of Healthy Start activities are provided to multiple-needs families, potentially involving case management or multidisciplinary service teams—the kind of context in which extensive outcome assessment would be appropriate and feasible. Thus, Healthy Start outcomes are measured for only a subset of Healthy Start participants: those most intensively served, as defined by individual sites. This means that the full range of impacts of all Healthy Start activities is not directly known for all individual participants. Only to the extent that schoolwide or large-group activities have an impact on schoolwide measures, such as the frequency of disciplinary actions and average daily attendance, will those effects be identified in the evaluation.

Confidentiality Concerns. All those involved in Healthy Start share a concern for the confidentiality of information collected about children and

Figure 4.2.   Distribution of Recorded Services Delivered

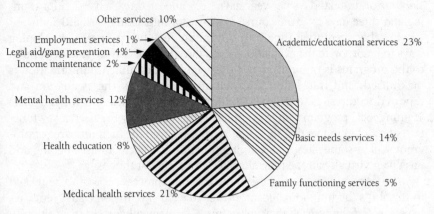

Other services 10%

Employment services 1%
Legal aid/gang prevention 4%
Income maintenance 2%

Academic/educational services 23%

Mental health services 12%

Health education 8%

Basic needs services 14%

Family functioning services 5%

Medical health services 21%

Note: n = 402,790 services recorded by 1992 and 1993 grantees through September 1994.

families. A statutory change in 1991 (Assembly Bill 2184) removed many potential barriers to information sharing by allowing collaborating agencies to share information relevant to a client's service plan. Nonetheless, at the outset, some local programs remained reluctant to report information that identified individuals or their outcomes to anyone outside the circle of immediate local service providers, including the evaluation team or the state partnership. Many sites have accommodated their confidentiality concerns by naming SRI or naming evaluation as a use of information on the informed consent forms they ask their case-managed clients to sign. Other programs have chosen to use identification numbers rather than names on data forms submitted to the evaluation. However, few programs have experience with such numerical identification systems and many have had tremendous difficulty ensuring that numbers are accurate, assigned in an unduplicated fashion to single individuals, and recorded on every data form sent to the evaluation. Thus, some data from some sites, particularly in the early months of the evaluation, could not be linked (for example, baseline measures to follow-up measures, services received to outcome achieved) and considerable site support has been needed to correct procedures. Some programs have even abandoned identification systems in the course of their evaluation experience.

Site Support. Given the scope of the evaluation's data needs and the variation in sites' willingness and ability to incorporate data-related procedures into their programs, the evaluation used an extensive program of site support related to evaluation. Each of the sixty-five sites in the evaluation has been provided a local evaluation coach. Coaches are professionals in or near each local community who have experience with evaluation in general and who have been hired, trained, and supervised by SRI to understand and communicate the needs of the Healthy Start evaluation to local sites. Thirty coaches served sixty-five sites in 1994, with individual coaches offering support in up to three sites each. Coaches have been expected to spend one-half day per month on site; two additional days per year have been allocated to each coach for training and three days over the course of a year for interacting with SRI staff.

Coaches spent their time with sites in fulfilling two purposes: developing ways to incorporate the evaluation needs into the programs so that disruption to the programs is minimized and the accuracy and utility of information is maximized, and translating information produced by the evaluation and reported to the sites into program improvement implications for the sites. Training local program staff to complete forms accurately has been a key function of coaches in meeting their first purpose. Given the high turnover of program staff at some sites, this training function has been almost ongoing and has taken virtually all the time allocated to coaches at those sites.

Not surprisingly, the success of the coaching process appears to be related to the skills the individual coach brings to each site. In some sites, coaches have successfully assisted their programs with many other tasks in addition to the evaluation, such as drafting job descriptions, helping to write local program reports, and locating potential sources of additional funding. The experience of other sites with their assigned coaches has been less positive, however. More effective coaches seem to be those with related program experience (for example, those who have social-work or public-health training in addition to general evaluation expertise), those who are culturally and linguistically well-matched to their sites, and those who are not overcommitted to other professional activities and can devote the full amount of time allocated to each site. Changes in the coaching process, such as reducing the number of sites to which they were assigned and placing greater emphasis on substantive as well as evaluation experience, were made after the first year of the evaluation to increase the effectiveness of the coaches selected and the ways they worked with sites.

Despite the unevenness of experience with coaches, they have proven invaluable for the evaluation. For some sites, only by having an on-site evaluation representative who would intervene directly with the program could any evaluation data be provided at all. Some coaches have abstracted evaluation data from client case files, collected school records that overworked or reluctant school staff did not provide, and picked up staff rosters for sampling purposes when they were not provided by participating schools. Coaches have helped to extend the reach of the SRI evaluation team into the large number of participating Healthy Start communities.

Responsiveness in Reporting. The evaluation team has an analysis and reporting agenda that is intended to respond to the variety of information needs and audiences of the initiative. Recognizing the central role of local sites in waging the Healthy Start battles to integrate services, formative evaluation information on individual sites has been reported to them quarterly. Each site has received a two-page report that summarizes the characteristics of clients served in the preceding quarter and year to date together with the number and variety of services that were provided to them directly by the program, or for which clients were wait-listed or referred to other agencies. This information, interpreted with the aid of their coaches, has helped local programs address such issues as whether they are serving the population they intend to serve, whether they have access to the range of services clients need, and whether the mix of services they provide directly is a good match to program goals and to client needs. Survey information on collaboration and service delivery processes also has been summarized for each site as it is compiled, and individual program outcomes will be reported to each program when all data are available at the conclusion of the evaluation.

At the initiative level, multiple reporting foci and formats also are apparent. For example, by early 1994, three major reports on the processes and evolution of collaborative planning and implementation had been produced (Wagner, 1994; Wagner and others, 1994a, 1994b; Golan, Kelley, and Wagner, 1995).

Outcomes were the focus of the report that was legislatively mandated to be submitted to the superintendent of public instruction by June of 1994 (Wagner and others, 1994a). As mentioned above, this meant that program participants who had enrollment and follow-up data had been enrolled only six months—perhaps not long enough to observe significant changes. The partnership and local sites experienced considerable anxiety in anticipating this report, fearing that the quick timetable might result in an absence of positive impacts, even if some of the local models eventually would be effective in improving client outcomes. It was a relief to these participants when early evaluation data showed positive outcomes in several domains.

At the conclusion of the evaluation, reports will summarize data on process and outcomes from the first three years of the initiative. In addition to these comprehensive reports, briefing memos have been prepared that frame findings on process and early outcomes in the context of issues specific to individual audiences (such as the legislature, school boards, and health and social service providers).

Early Outcomes

The interim outcomes reported to the superintendent and legislature in 1994 were based on data submitted by only twenty-nine of the first forty operational grantees—the only sites that had been serving clients long enough for them to have six-month follow-up measures to compare to intake status so that change could be determined. Approximately three hundred family units and several multiply served individuals made up the sample on which outcome measurement was based at this early stage. The sample varied by outcome measure, as noted previously. It was as large as 1,200 individuals for measures taken for all clients at all sites. For mental health measures, which were used only by programs with a mental health focus, 700 individuals were measured, whereas student grades were obtained for 270 students (one child in each multiply served family). Clients were pooled across sites, without regard to the site from which they were drawn. Only when the evaluation is complete will it be clear whether six-month outcomes from these initial samples of clients differ from the outcomes assessed over a longer period for a larger population in many more sites.

Figure 4.3 summarizes selected early outcomes for families and children in the areas of basic needs, health care, and mental health status for the initial group of clients; statistically significant gains are noted in all areas. Grade point averages also improved for children participating in Healthy Start, particularly for elementary school students and for those who were performing least well before their involvement in the program. For example, GPAs improved for students in the lowest grade quartile from 1.26 before their Healthy Start experience to 1.47 later ($p < .05$), and the average grades for elementary school students increased from 1.97 to 2.07 ($p < .01$).

Statistically significant changes were not demonstrated in some other measures, such as the number of out-of-home placements, use of emergency rooms for nonemergency medical care, and the rate at which children had a "medical home." Further, only one statistically significant school-level improvement was noted midway through the first grant year for the 118 schools included in the initial subset of 29 sites that reported early outcome data: the average number of disciplinary actions per month declined by thirty-two, as reported by principals in participating schools.

Despite the preliminary and mixed nature of these findings, the overall results were judged positive enough that the legislature and governor were willing to continue support for the initiative.

Summary

This discussion has outlined the complexities of policy, politics, finances, and logistics that form the context for one of the nation's largest school-linked services initiatives, California's Healthy Start. It also has depicted the choices made by the partners in the initiative and its evaluators in striking a balance between evaluation rigor and the contextual realities they face. The lessons embodied in and drawn from those choices are intended to be instructive to evaluators, practitioners, funders, and policy makers as we all observe and engage in the revolution in service integration occurring around us.

Not all challenges to the validity of the evaluation results have been overcome in the present context of Healthy Start, and many choices have required reconsideration as experience has taught participants increasingly more about how such a large-scale initiative is implemented and how it can, and cannot, be evaluated. Failures thus far in perfecting our evaluation craft in the context of integrated services should not be allowed to deter our field from applying what we know to this new and challenging arena. Policy decisions will be made regarding service integration, whether or not evaluation data are available. Those decisions will be better made if they are informed by the best evaluation data possible given the current state of our craft, accompanied by clear statements regarding what can and cannot be concluded from them. Growing

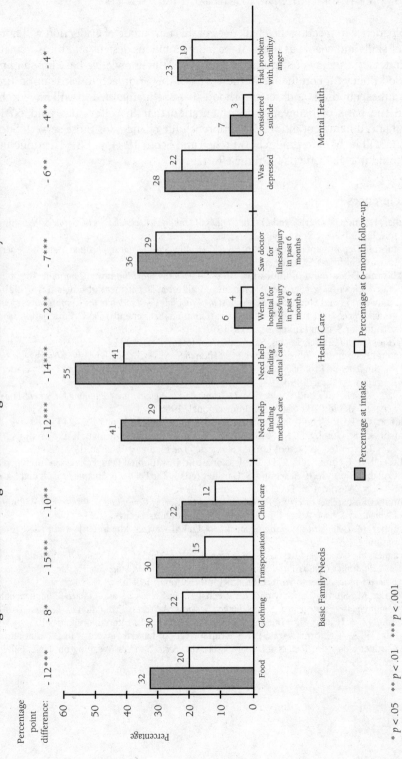

Figure 4.3. Selected Significant Changes in Outcomes for Healthy Start Core Clients

* $p < .05$ ** $p < .01$ *** $p < .001$

66   EVALUATING INITIATIVES TO INTEGRATE HUMAN SERVICES

experience in meeting the challenges of this new mode of evaluation will hone
our skills and enable us to reach for more ambitious designs and measurement
strategies, thereby continuing to strengthen the knowledge base for shaping
good policy. "If confidence in the virtue of this approach toward supporting
families, children, and neighborhoods is to be maintained, it will have to be
on the basis of believable documentation that the effort has paid off in
enhanced living conditions and improved life chances for those served. Such
data will be hard to produce" (Mitchell and Scott, 1994, p. 88). The difficulty
should not dissuade us from the effort.

References

Adler, L., and Gardner, S. (eds.). *The Politics of Linking Schools and Social Services.* Washington, D.C.: Falmer Press, 1994.
California Department of Education. *SB 620/Healthy Start Grant Application Materials.* Sacramento: California Department of Education, 1992a.
California Department of Education. *SB 620—Healthy Start Initiative. Comprehensive, Integrated School-Linked Services.* Sacramento: California Department of Education, 1992b.
Chynoweth, J., and Henderson, J. *Request for Proposals: Evaluation of the Comprehensive Integrated School-Linked Services Initiative in California.* Sacramento, Calif.: Foundation Consortium for School-Linked Services, 1992.
Dryfoos, J. *Full-Service Schools.* San Francisco: Jossey-Bass, 1994.
General Accounting Office. *School-Linked Human Services: A Comprehensive Strategy for Aiding Students at Risk of School Failure.* GAO/HRD-94-21. Washington, D.C.: General Accounting Office, 1993.
Golan, S., Kelley, F., and Wagner, M. *Developments in Collaborative Planning for School-Linked Services.* Menlo Park, Calif.: SRI International, 1995.
Larson, C. (ed.). "School-Linked Services." *The Future of Children,* 1992, 2 (1).
Larson, C. S., Gomby, D. S., Shiono, P. H., Lewit, E. M., and Behrman, R. E. "Analysis." In C. S. Larson (ed.), "School-Linked Services," *The Future of Children,* 1992, 2 (1).
Mitchell, D. E., and Scott, L. D. "Professional and Institutional Perspectives on Interagency Collaboration." In L. Adler and S. Gardner (eds.), *The Politics of Linking Schools and Social Services.* Washington, D.C.: Falmer Press, 1994.
Philliber Research Associates. *An Evaluation of the Caring Communities Program at Walbridge Elementary School.* Accord, N.Y.: Philliber Research Associates, 1994.
Wagner, M. *Collaborative Planning for School-Linked Services.* Menlo Park, Calif.: SRI International, 1994.
Wagner, M., Golan, S., Shaver, D., Newman, L., Wechsler, M., and Kelley, F. *A Healthy Start for California's Children and Families: Early Findings from a Statewide Evaluation of School-Linked Services.* Menlo Park, Calif.: SRI International, 1994a.
Wagner, M., Shaver, D., Newman, L., Wechsler, M., Kelley, F., and Golan, S. *Implementing Comprehensive, Integrated, School-Linked Services: A Process Evaluation of the First Year of California's Healthy Start Initiative.* Menlo Park, Calif.: SRI International, 1994b.
White, W. A. "California's State Partnership for School-Linked Services." In L. Adler and S. Gardner (eds.), *The Politics of Linking Schools and Social Services.* Washington, D.C.: Falmer Press, 1994.

MARY M. WAGNER is program director for education and human services research at SRI International. She is principal investigator for the statewide evaluation of California's Healthy Start initiative.

DEANNA S. GOMBY is director of research and grants for child development at the Center for the Future of Children of The David and Lucile Packard Foundation. The foundation joined the Foundation Consortium for School-Linked Services in 1994.

*The methodology and findings of two Colorado studies are described,
followed by a synthesis of both evaluations and how they contribute to
lessons learned in evaluating state-level services integration initiatives.*

Evaluation of State-Level Integrated Services Initiatives: Colorado's Experience

Donna M. Garnett, Marsha S. Gould

There is general consensus that better results for families and children would
occur if human services in a community were integrated rather than fragmented. The bulk of the literature on integrated services focuses on the service
delivery level—the interface between the consumer and the provider (Coulton,
1992; Kahn and Kamerman, 1992; Young and others, 1994). In order to suc-
ceed and become institutionalized, however, integration efforts on the service
delivery level must be supported by policy changes at the state level.

State agencies serve as conduits to communities for federal programs and
resources, and also implement and monitor state and federal rules and regulations governing the expenditure of funds and delivery of services. State-level
barriers such as reporting requirements and confidentiality statutes can often
impede community services integration initiatives. Disbursement of state programs across multiple agencies can make integrating services in the community even more difficult.

The question for those interested in achieving services integration is where
to begin. Does one assume that when a community encounters obstacles to
service system integration it pressures the state to change? Or does community services integration occur when the state changes policy to force compliance or provide incentives? Are both directions of pressure for change
necessary for services integration to occur?

Kagan and others (1995) provide a useful conceptual framework for view-
ing this interrelationship between local service delivery and state-level systems
integration efforts. They identify four distinct approaches: client-centered,

program-centered, policy-centered, and organization-centered. Client-centered approaches focus on the point of interaction between client and provider. Program-centered approaches create linkages between agencies and programs so that services for clients can be improved. Policy-centered approaches are government attempts to forge connections throughout the human services system, across agencies, and at state and local levels. Organization-centered approaches to services integration involve reconfiguring or restructuring government agencies. Presumably, client- and program-centered approaches could take place at the service delivery or community level, but policy- and organization-centered approaches require broader state-level support.

Evaluation of Two State-Level Services Integration Efforts

This chapter reviews the initial evaluations of two Colorado services integration efforts, the State Efforts in Early Childhood (SEEC) Management Team and the Family Centers Initiative. These two initiatives have developed against the backdrop of a major restructuring of the state's human services. The Family Centers Initiative was designed to stimulate and support community-level system integration efforts with the expectation that this could inform and stimulate state changes. The SEEC Team, on the other hand, brought together representatives of multiple state agencies serving families and young children to change state policy, which would in turn facilitate and reinforce community system integration efforts.

Kagan and others (1995) use the two Colorado projects cited above in one of their case studies. They identify Family Centers as a program-centered approach, whereas the SEEC Team is considered policy-centered. They also consider the overall human services restructuring as an organization-centered approach to services integration.

These two projects and Colorado's current restructuring effort are the direct outgrowth of Colorado's *Strategic Plan for Families and Children,* released in 1990. Based on a documented deterioration in the status of families and children during the 1980s, the plan delineated several policy goals to improve the multiple systems of state government that administer services to at-risk families and children. Those goals include shifting to outcome-oriented accountability systems; integrating the state budget to maximize all funding sources; increasing prevention efforts; ensuring that state policies, practices, rules, and regulations have a positive impact on family functioning; making service delivery more efficient and effective by providing a single point for access to services; and training the human services work force to work collaboratively with each other in partnership with families.

The plan served as a springboard for several systems reform initiatives, which were launched nearly simultaneously. As a first step, a Commission on Families and Children was established by executive order. The commission was made up of child and family advocates from the nonprofit sector, business leaders, cabinet members at the state and county levels, and families. During its two-year existence, the commission developed the Family Centers Initiative and the cabinet members on the commission formed an initial steering committee for a major restructuring of the state's human services. Restructuring was viewed as a way to integrate policies and budgets and as a more effective and efficient means of administering the state's human services. Cabinet members on the restructuring steering committee anticipated that the scope and political sensitivity of the restructuring effort meant that desired policy changes might be a long time coming. Therefore, the cabinet members recommended that a parallel but related integration effort be launched around the issues of early childhood. Ultimately, this recommendation led to the formation in 1991 of the SEEC Team.

The evaluations of these two projects were not initially designed as parts of a single study. But there are substantial parallels in the lessons that can be learned and the conclusions that can be drawn; therefore, they are considered together here. The SEEC Team evaluation looked at the context into which proposed state policy changes would be introduced. The Family Center evaluation examined the degree to which the processes of establishing family centers moved communities closer to the achievement of state goals for services integration.

Service integration efforts, whether at the service delivery or state level, are means as well as ends in themselves (Knapp, 1995). The goal of such efforts is a change in the way human services are delivered and financed in order to achieve an improvement in indicators of family, child, and individual well-being. Kagan and others (1995) refer to the two types of results from services integration as systemic accomplishments (such as changes in policy, program, staff development, and funding) and outcomes for children and families (such as reductions in teen births or poverty and increases in high school graduation or early prenatal care).

The two Colorado evaluations discussed here occurred too early in the projects to look at outcomes for families and children. The focus of these evaluations was on gathering baseline information and delineating systemic accomplishments.

Evaluation Issues

Several questions must be addressed in state-level evaluations. Does one evaluate success at the state level through a review of state changes in funding, policies, and demographic indicators of well-being, or should one infer state-level success from individual, local-level evaluations? Should state-level evaluations be formative or summative? Is there a legitimate rationale for using both qualitative and quantitative approaches to state-level evaluation? Is there a benefit to the use of self-evaluations by program administrators?

The authors conclude that state systems integration efforts must be evaluated on multiple dimensions: state policy and financing, community programs and demographic outcomes, service provider practices, and consumer satisfaction and perception. The evaluations discussed in this chapter cover all of these aspects to some extent.

Both evaluations considered here were formative in that they occurred early in the process and provided feedback to inform the continuing development of the service integration efforts (Herman, Morris, and Fitz-Gibbon, 1989). The evaluations described here were qualitative in nature because they focused on gaining an understanding of contexts and processes. The outcomes were of a systemic nature and were not clearly defined, also indicating the need for a qualitative approach (Herman, Morris, and Fitz-Gibbon, 1989).

Despite the focus of these evaluations, the authors support the notion that state-level evaluation of services integration readily lends itself to a combination of quantitative and qualitative approaches (Reichardt and Rallis, 1994; Knapp, 1995). Examples of potential quantitative approaches to evaluate the effectiveness of a state-level services integration initiative are tracking outcomes or indicators of child and family well-being or conducting a budget trend analysis to document changes in spending for prevention and early intervention.

Even the interpretation of quantitative results, however, demands an understanding of the context in which they occurred. For example, if the data in a given year indicate a decline in the number of reported cases of child abuse and neglect, the researcher must understand what other changes, such as changes in reporting or investigation requirements, could account for a reduction in child abuse reports. "Quite simply, researchers cannot benefit from the use of numbers if they do not know, in common sense terms, what the numbers mean" (Reichardt and Cook, 1979, p. 23).

Self-evaluation as a tool in state-level evaluation is often considered less rigorous than an independent evaluation conducted by a third party. In the Colorado studies, self-evaluation was used in conjunction with an external evaluation to enable communities to check their perceptions against those of outside evaluators and thereby address their internal issues. In reality, few human service providers are familiar or comfortable with evaluation, and building a tradition of self-evaluation is an important element in any systems integration effort (Cohen and Ooms, 1993).

Evaluation of the State Efforts in Early Childhood Management Team

The SEEC Team was formed in 1991 to create a more effective, comprehensive, integrated, family-centered service delivery system. The team is made up of management-level representatives from several state agencies, including education, human services, mental health, health, and higher education that administer, deliver, and fund programs and services for children prenatally through age eight. The authors were commissioned to conduct a baseline analysis of the state's early childhood services system.

A variety of qualitative methods were used to collect the evaluation data. These included a review and analysis of existing policy documents from multiple state agencies, a survey of state agency program managers, interviews with state agency program directors, and focus groups with local service providers and parents as consumers of early childhood services. In addition, the analysis included reviewing changes in key indicators for children and families in Colorado from 1990 to the present in order to trace demographic trends in areas such as child poverty, infant mortality, teen births, child immunizations, deaths from child abuse, and low-birth-weight rates.

Review and Analysis of Policy Documents. As a collaborative governing structure, the SEEC Team adopted the vision for young children and their families put forth by the 1990 *Strategic Plan* and articulated a set of principles to guide state agencies that provide programs and services for young children and their families:

Agencies should work in partnership with parents in all levels of decision making.

State agencies should focus on prevention and early intervention.

Certain core services should be available to all young children.

Funding should be determined by a child's and family's multiple needs rather than by programs.

State agencies should build on strengths and support family functioning.

People who work with young children and their families must have specific skills.

Decisions about services for young children should involve collaborative partners at all levels of government and across all systems.

Although these principles provided general guidance, they were not further defined or specified, thus increasing the challenge for evaluators in using them as criteria for measuring achievement.

The evaluators reviewed the key policy documents of each state agency and compared those documents with the stated principles of the SEEC Management Team. In all, documents from sixty-three programs in six departments were reviewed. All of the programs included in the review incorporated language into their written policy documents and program descriptions that was compatible with many of the SEEC principles. However, no single program or agency incorporated all of the principles into its written documents. A review of programs and budgets to determine whether practices actually reflected these principles found that none were fully operationalized, and those involving significant funding, such as the provision of core services, were not operationalized at all.

Demographic Trend Data. Trends on key indicators were reviewed in conjunction with the evaluation. The SEEC Team adopted a set of indicators developed through a statewide advocacy movement to improve child outcomes by the year 2000. The status of these indicators is published each year through the *KIDSCOUNT in COLORADO!* publication. Between 1988, when baseline data were first collected, and 1992, the most current data available, child poverty, low-birth-weight rate, teen births, and deaths from child abuse all increased. Infant mortality decreased and the percentage of immunized children under two years increased. In addition to the indicators described above, the SEEC Team has identified three additional outcomes for young children: to increase the number of young children who enter school with appropriate readiness skills, to increase the percentage of children who enter fourth grade with appropriate language and social skills, and to decrease the number of infants born substance-addicted or with HIV/AIDS. No direct measures of these outcomes currently exist.

Survey of State Agency Program Managers. A written questionnaire was sent to program managers in all state agencies that provide services and programs for young children. The purpose of the questionnaire was to ascertain the sources and amounts of funds being used to help young children and to identify the numbers of children being served with each source of funds. Respondents were also asked to indicate the basis on which funding decisions are made for each funding stream (federal or state formula funding, child need, performance accountability) and to indicate how program effectiveness is evaluated.

Analysis showed that most of the funding streams are dictated by categorical funding requirements established at the state and federal levels. In only a few instances are resources available to follow the child's needs. State-funded programs almost never include funding for program administration or evaluation. Basically, funding decisions are not made on the basis of performance. A notable exception in the area of evaluation is the state's preschool program for four- and five-year-olds at risk of later school failure. Funded by sources other than the state general fund, these evaluations have demonstrated the effectiveness of this program in mitigating certain risk factors such as poor language development. As a result, this program is consistently supported in the legislature and efforts to expand the program have been highly successful.

Interviews with State Agency Program Directors. Interviews were conducted with sixteen managers of state programs that affect young children and their families to ascertain their perceptions of the elements of an ideal system of care for Colorado's young children. Interviewees were asked to describe their ideal system of early childhood care, education, and support, and to describe existing barriers to that ideal. In the ideal, such a system would be comprehensive and would reflect family-centered values, and multiple agencies would work together to improve child and family outcomes. Some of the barriers reported by the interviewees include the following: parents are not sufficiently included in decision making, categorical funding streams drive single-focused programming, many decisions about services to families and children are made on the basis of income eligibility and categorical restrictions rather than on the basis of what children and families need, and communication mechanisms within and across agencies are not well-linked. Interviewees further expressed concern that policies set at the state and federal levels to support integrated service delivery are often compromised at the middle-management and program delivery levels.

Regardless of agency, funding authority, or level of responsibility, the administrators consistently described a system of care that was remarkably congruent with the stated principles of the SEEC Team. State-level administrators, however, were less likely to see barriers at the state level than were local-level users of the system.

Focus Group Discussions with Users. An important component of the evaluation involved getting the perspective of users of the state's system of care for young children. Separate focus groups were held with parents and local service providers in representative areas of the state. Parents were asked about the quality, appropriateness, accessibility, and coordination of services as well as their perceptions of their relationships with service providers. Providers were asked about the extent of collaboration in their community, barriers to community collaboration, and the relationship between their agency and state services.

Several agencies on the SEEC Team have made considerable effort to streamline many bureaucratic hurdles, such as those associated with child care licensing. However, the general perception of users of the system (both consumers and local service providers) continues to be that state agencies are unresponsive and intractable. Other barriers to a more effective, integrated, and family-friendly service delivery system cited by users included lack of ongoing funding for innovative programs, inaccessibility of state program managers to assist in planning and implementation efforts in the more isolated rural areas of the state, lack of assistance for local efforts to set and evaluate goals and outcomes, and communication problems. Focus group participants reported that lack of collaboration at the state level in setting funding priorities, monitoring, and policy making was one of the biggest barriers to local efforts to integrate services.

Conclusions. Several conclusions can be drawn from the evaluation. First, the program managers in the various state agencies that make up the state's system of care for young children strongly support collaborative models of decision making and integration of services at the local level. Across the system, many examples of cooperation, coordination, and collaboration can be found. However, few formal mechanisms exist to sustain the collaborative approach and integration of services. A real strength of the system is the quality of the working relationships among the existing program managers.

A challenge to state agencies is to maintain the collaborative relationships and commitments to programs in the face of other systems change initiatives, such as restructuring of state human services and proposed federal block grants. Ironically, as funding for state-funded, prevention-oriented, collaborative programs increases, there may be less motivation to pool existing resources for these collaborative endeavors. Under federal block grant proposals, the incentives to work together in providing integrated services may be negated as prevention programs and traditional categorical programs vie for severely reduced resources (for example, family support programs that are funded under the same block grant as foster care).

Second, virtually no resources exist for evaluating the effectiveness of prevention efforts, which means that very few data exist to support the rationale for the funding of prevention and early intervention efforts. In a changing policy environment that demands results, this lack of documented effectiveness puts many early childhood programs and services at risk for significant funding cuts.

Third, a significant amount of resources (federal and state) are allocated to young children and their families. However, little effort goes into combining these funding streams to provide a comprehensive package of services for young children and their families. Innovative use of funds from multiple agencies to support integrated services projects such as family centers (described in the next section) are short-lived in nature and generally support planning and startup without funding long-term operations. Traditional, single-focused programs continue to be funded, whereas prevention-oriented, integrated approaches must pursue funding through multiple sources such as grants from the private sector.

Evaluation of the Family Centers Initiative

The Colorado Family Centers Initiative was conceived as a laboratory for operationalizing the systems integration goals set forth in the *Strategic Plan for Families and Children*. Family centers were described as "multi-agency, collaborative efforts to provide comprehensive, intensive, integrated and community-based services to families and children at risk" (p. 37). In 1992, the governor's office announced the first of three waves of planning and startup grants to launch family centers as integrated services pilot programs. This section details the process evaluation of the first wave of projects during their first year of operation, conducted as a way of framing the progress of the state in achieving its own goals for systemic reform.

The family centers in the first wave of the initiative were selected through a competitive process under the guidance of the Commission on Families and Children and administered by the governor's office. Communities responded to a call for proposals that required multiple public and private organizations to work together to design a family center that would address a set of basic principles agreed on by the commission. These principles reflect many of the principles of family support programs advanced by Coulton (1992). Such programs are family-centered, neighborhood-based, voluntary, and culturally appropriate, and involve consumers in all phases of policy and program development.

Family centers were also expected to address fourteen desired components: clearly delineating community problems affecting families and children, articulating a shared vision and values, describing clear and specific goals to be achieved, providing services at a neighborhood level, focusing on the whole family, incorporating a single point of entry, providing case management through a family advocate, integrating multiple services at the family center location, using a family assessment to determine needs, including families as equal partners, ensuring cultural competence of staff, outreaching to families of diverse circumstances, using cross-agency collaboration, and evaluating outcomes in relation to the identified problems affecting families and children.

In keeping with Colorado's strong adherence to a philosophy of local control, family centers were expected to be customized to meet the needs of their communities. Within that context, the community's family center plan had to clearly delineate problems affecting families and children, articulate a shared vision and values, and describe clear and specific goals to be achieved. The model of service delivery could take many forms but had to exhibit the characteristics of a neighborhood-based, family-centered, integrated services approach incorporating a single point of entry and case management through a family advocate. Other components to be addressed were the use of a family assessment, inclusion of families as equal partners, cultural competence of staff, and active outreach to families of diverse circumstances. Family centers were expected to be the products of cross-agency collaboration and were expected to evaluate outcomes in relation to the identified problems affecting families and children.

Eight communities were selected in the first wave and represented urban and rural communities throughout the state. Ultimately, one community dropped out of the initiative and one community received minimal funding to carry out a different purpose. Consequently, six communities were the subject of the evaluation.

All but one of the centers were located in high-risk communities where poverty, crime, poor housing, and unemployment are significant. Family centers operated under a variety of auspices. Some were located in schools, two were in recreation centers, and others operated under multipurpose community centers. Community planning teams participated in a six-month structured planning process to design their family center plans. The funding levels, which ranged between $50,000 and $175,000, were determined on the basis of those plans. Family centers in the second and third waves were also selected through a competitive process, but the planning and implementation processes were modified and oversight was moved to the Colorado Department of Human Services. These family centers were not included in this evaluation.

The evaluation design included reviewing each family center plan in relation to the state goals for family centers as part of a larger systems reform effort. Interviews were conducted on-site with members of the original planning team, the director of the center, and members of the existing governance structure. Follow-up site visits were conducted to observe the actual programs and activities of the center and to interview staff members and families (consumers) participating in the center. In addition to the evaluations conducted by the evaluators, the family center director and governing board completed a self-assessment instrument.

Although the ultimate purpose of the family centers is to improve child and family outcomes, the question of outcomes was not addressed in the first-year evaluation. In many ways this is the most salient—perhaps the only—question to be posed. However, the evaluators determined that a focus on outcomes was premature because the centers had been operational for only a few months when the evaluation began.

This evaluation looked at the process by which family centers moved from the planning stage to implementation and the degree to which family centers achieved the program goals they had set for themselves, in line with desired expectations established by the state. In particular, the evaluation explained the extent to which family centers were family-friendly and were able to function as sources of integrated services. The formative nature of the evaluation was useful in identifying where the family centers were not achieving the desired components set by the state or where they were falling short of their own family center plan.

In-Depth Interviews. During the first phase of the evaluation project, site visits were made by a three-person evaluation team over two days. The number of interviews conducted at each center ranged from ten to twenty-seven. In addition, the evaluators toured each family center and observed one or more activities of the center. Before the first site visit, the evaluators reviewed the original state documents describing the family center initiative, the funded implementation plan for each center, and existing forms, brochures, quarterly reports, and other written materials related to each center.

In general, those interviewed were remarkably consistent in their understanding of the purpose and goals of the family center. In only one location were members of the current governing committee unable to articulate the purpose and goals of the family center. This seems to indicate that in most centers a commitment to the original vision of the family center remained in place.

Almost all those interviewed responded that the family centers had not yet lived up to their expectations, but all indicated that meeting those expectations was within the realm of possibility, given time and adequate resources. A frustration reported by interviewees in all family centers was the issue of inadequate funding. In all cases the funding proposed in order to fulfill the community family center plan had been reduced by the state. Other perceived challenges of family centers during the startup phase of implementation included lack of consensus among collaborators, turf issues across agencies, lack of focus on outcomes, lack of clarity about roles, and failure to make financial commitments among the collaborators. The perceived strengths at the point of implementation seemed to be commitment of the planning team, involvement of the community, key leader support, a strong program director, and effective family advocates who are capable of helping families meet basic needs and improve family functioning.

In addition to analyzing the interviews, the evaluators rated the family centers on each of the fourteen desired or key components discussed above. Each component was rated as "not observed," "has not met expectations," "has met expectations," or "has exceeded expectations." The evaluators assigned the ratings on the basis of the interviews, reviews of quarterly reports, and observations of family center activities. Three centers were meeting or exceeding more than 70 percent of the expectations. One center was meeting or exceeding between 50 percent and 70 percent, and two centers were meeting or exceeding expectations on less than 50 percent of the key components. The expectation about a family-centered approach was almost always met or exceeded; the expectations about a single point of entry and service integration were most often rated as "has not met expectations." It may have been premature to expect that the family centers would have achieved the goal of service integration, given that most of the centers had only been operational for a few months. None of the centers had collected data related to specific child and family outcomes.

Parent Focus Groups. A second set of site visits was conducted approximately six months after the initial interviews. A trained focus group facilitator conducted parent focus groups in each of the six communities. Families were asked to describe their involvement in the family center, how they felt families were involved in the operation of the center, and how the family center had made an impact on their lives. Family center directors were asked to arrange the focus groups. They were urged to invite ten to twelve families, representing diverse circumstances, who had received services from the family center programs to participate in the focus groups.

In all, thirty-three family members participated in the focus group discussions. Ninety percent of the participants were mothers. Participants were representative of the cultural diversity of their communities and the state.

Parents in five of the six centers had received some type of crisis intervention or assistance in meeting basic needs. Examples of crisis intervention included helping families find emergency housing or get medical treatment, and loaning parents small sums of money (under $100) to pay for transportation to a job interview or to pay registration for a job training program. In most of the centers, focus group participants reported that they had taken part in social events and their children had participated in educational or child care programs.

Parents described the most significant impact of the family center on their lives in terms of emotional support, skills development, reduced isolation, and the opportunity to give back to the community. For the most part, families viewed the family centers as having a positive influence on their lives.

Observations of Representative Activities. During the second site visit, an evaluator observed representative activities sponsored by the family center. In an attempt to keep the observations as objective as possible, another independent evaluator was hired. The evaluator was not allowed to read any reports from the first site visit before making the observations. The evaluator used an open-ended observation protocol that examined the purpose of the activity, the level of participation by family members, and the quality of the interaction between family center staff and the participants.

When comparing the observations with the interview summaries from the first site visit, the issues identified during the first site visit were nearly identical to those identified by the other independent evaluator during the second site visit. This suggests that problems established early in the process have a way of continuing long into the implementation phase.

In general, the family center activities exhibited family-friendly qualities. Examples of these qualities were evident in the responsive attitudes of the family advocates and other staff. The centers appeared to serve families from diverse situations and offer a nonstigmatized environment. Three of the family centers were clearly hubs of activity in the community and many families were coming and going easily throughout the center. These centers incorporated many parents as volunteers, staff, and advisors and all three had been operating programs and services for families and children for a year or more.

Self-Evaluations. The fourth component of the evaluation project included a self-evaluation completed by the center director and approved by the governance board of each center. The self-evaluation instrument was developed specifically for this evaluation project and was based on the original call for proposals released by the governor's office. The evaluation instrument included open-ended questions asking for examples of how the fourteen desired key components listed above were being met and for checklists and ratings on each of the components.

Several questions on the self-evaluation instrument were aimed at the essential elements associated with integrated services. For example, one question asked respondents to describe how services are integrated. Three centers indicated that they refer families to other services in the community. Only one of those centers actually makes it possible for families to apply for needed services through the center. Three centers make services such as Women, Infants, and Children benefits and immunization clinics available at the site on a periodic basis. One center indicated that they offer multiple services at the family center site, one center jointly trained staff from multiple agencies that participate in the activities of the center, and two centers plan jointly with other agencies.

Another question relevant to integrated services asked which programs or agencies participate with the family center in actually delivering services to families and children and the frequency with which these partners participate. On the basis of self-report, it appears that public health, mental health, recreation, parent education agencies, and elementary schools are the entities most likely to be involved in delivering services in conjunction with the family center. During earlier interviews, most of the family center directors expressed some difficulty in working with the county social services department.

In the area of pooled funds, only two family centers indicated that the collaborating agencies combine funding streams on behalf of the center. Several of the centers are accessing other public sources of funds, but these are primarily secured through the submittal of a grant to a state agency and not through any institutionalized redeployment of resources. All six centers indicated that they rely on outside grants in order to sustain the center and some centers have been able to leverage private dollars. However, no family centers described a scenario where existing dollars such as those associated with case management, eligibility determination, or treatment were now being rerouted through the center.

With the exception of one center, all the family centers rated themselves considerably higher overall on the key components than they were rated by the evaluators. Several reasons may account for the difference. Because the self-evaluation was conducted several months after the first on-site visit, it is possible that the centers had made tremendous progress toward achieving the components. A likelier possibility is that the psychological effects of seeing one's own work in a positive light due to personal investment may account for the discrepancy.

The self-evaluation instrument also included questions related to improved child and family outcomes as stated in the overall purpose of the family centers. Respondents were asked to list each of the identified problems targeted by the family center, to rate the level of effectiveness of the center in addressing the problems, and to indicate what methods of evaluation were used to arrive at that rating.

The family centers identified a myriad of problems, including poor school achievement, poor health outcomes, inadequate parenting, and teen pregnancy. However, most of the centers responded that they do not know whether their efforts are effective at addressing the identified problems. At the time of the evaluation project, none of the centers were using any quantitative, objective methods to assess their impact.

Conclusions. Several conclusions emerge from the family centers evaluation. First, the planning period is critical for creating a shared vision and for forging a working coalition committed to carrying out that vision. Unresolved issues during the planning period are magnified very quickly as the centers attempt to move into the implementation phase.

Second, family centers experience a transition period between the planning and implementation phases, during which time a center may appear to flounder and lose ground. Significant technical support is needed during this time to enable successful negotiation of the transition period.

Third, Colorado's family centers have not yet achieved the desired service delivery model of integrated services implied by the recommended components. Some of the barriers to implementing this approach include rigid policies and procedures and the still-fragmented funding structures at the state level. Barriers such as turfism and unwillingness to redeploy resources at the local level inhibit the implementation of integrated services as well. Clearly, integrated services as envisioned by the *Strategic Plan* are difficult to achieve. This difficulty stems from the inherent challenges associated with collaboration and from the lack of a clear definition of integrated services.

As can be learned from the family centers evaluation, gradations of integrated services exist (see Konrad, this volume). For example, integrated services can mean that multiple services are co-located at the single location of the family center, each retaining its separate funding, authority, and accountability. Another model might consist of multiple funding streams pooled in a common fund to support various family center services. Staff associated with different agencies work as a multidisciplinary team and policy, budget, and program decisions are made jointly by the collaborators (consumers as well as agencies) in the family center. These gradations pose critical questions for evaluation. For example, is one dimension more effective in producing improved outcomes for children and families? Under what conditions can each level of integrated services be achieved?

Synthesis of the Two Evaluations

Although conducted under different auspices and focused on different approaches to services integration, the evaluations of the SEEC Team and the Family Centers Initiative combined provide a picture of Colorado's context for and early efforts at services integration. It is clear that state- and local-level services integration efforts can and do occur simultaneously. The goals of the SEEC Team and the Family Centers Initiative were to operationalize family-friendly or family-supportive principles. Both state-level and community-level projects were designed to achieve comprehensive, coordinated services to improve outcomes for children and families. This discussion looks at the findings of both evaluations to draw some conclusions about the degree to which Colorado's projects were successful at achieving these goals.

Both Colorado projects did a good job of articulating and emphasizing family support. The language of most state documents stresses parental involvement in all levels of planning and decision making. Family members were involved in the activities of the centers and felt their participation was valued. At some centers, however, board members who were both agency representatives and parents felt their participation was sufficient to fulfill the desired component of parental and consumer involvement, even though they were not actually consumers of family center services.

Colorado has many examples of services integration efforts, primarily in the areas of joint planning and pooled funding at the state level and co-location of services at the community level. For the most part, however, barriers to services integration have yet to be overcome. Turf protection, categorical funding, and competition for scarce resources all work against collaborative efforts to achieve service integration.

Colorado, like most states, has an "I'll know it when I see it" approach to operationalization of the construct of services integration. In both evaluations, analysis included examining whether principles or components of services integration had been achieved. In reality, however, the state should achieve some degree of consensus on how services integration will be defined so that participating entities can be held accountable.

Another area needing consensus is the assumption that services integration is a means to achieve the goal of improved outcomes for children and families. In the evaluations discussed in this chapter, progress toward services integration is documented, but whether it makes any difference in terms of better child outcomes is not.

Although Colorado appears to be clear about the direction it wants to go, it is far from reaching that destination. It does a reasonably good job of involving consumers and moving toward a family-centered approach. It is still struggling to find the money for prevention and early intervention. It does not focus on outcomes. Achieving optimum services integration remains in Colorado, as in most other states, an elusive goal.

Lessons Learned About Evaluation of State-Level Integrated Services Initiatives

Given the contemporary climate on the federal level and the specter of reduced funding and increased restrictions, it becomes especially important to evaluate services integration efforts for families and children. The experiences in Colorado have taught us that this is no simple task. A number of lessons have been learned that could benefit other state-level evaluations.

First, it is crucial to evaluate both process and outcomes. Although it is important to know what services integration mechanisms have evolved and why, this is a moot question unless some improvement occurs in the outcomes that stimulated the services integration effort in the first place. Second, it is imperative that definitions of key concepts such as services integration and family support be operationalized before implementation or an evaluation begins. What appears to be a common definition will evaporate quickly if a locality is rated poorly on a concept.

Third, most evaluations focus on success or failure. However, it is important to determine what distinguishes between successful and unsuccessful efforts. One factor, often overlooked but certainly crucial, is the quality of the relationships between the actors in any collaborative undertaking, whether at the state or local level. A history of trust and working together can be particularly critical to whether a services integration effort is successful.

Fourth, most evaluations are static processes. They paint a picture of a point in time. However, all collaborations and services integration efforts are developmental. Some points in the development of the effort, such as the transition phase, are often difficult. It is important, therefore, to clarify results of an evaluation within an understanding of the developmental process. The dynamic process associated with a formative evaluation is especially relevant in integrated services projects.

Fifth, service providers are more concerned with delivering a service than evaluating its impact. They operate from a premise that if there is a problem, it is always better to do something rather than nothing. Therefore, it is especially important in the case of services integration projects to consider the relevance of evaluation results for the entire range of audiences.

Finally, state-level evaluations have many different stakeholders. Legislators want to make informed policy and funding decisions. Administrators want to plan for programs and staffing. Front-line workers want to know when they have done a good job. Consumers want some assurance that their concerns are being addressed. Therefore, state-level evaluations must be planned and implemented, and the results disseminated, with these diverse audiences in mind.

References

Cohen, E., and Ooms, T. *Data Integration and Evaluation: Essential Components of Family-Centered Systems Reform.* Washington, D.C.: American Association for Marriage and Family Therapy Research and Education Foundation, 1993.

Colorado Children's Campaign. *KIDSCOUNT in COLORADO!* Denver: Colorado Children's Campaign, 1994.

Colorado Strategic Plan for Families and Children. Denver: Governor's Office, 1990.

Coulton, C. "Framework for Evaluating Family Centers." Unpublished paper, Case Western Reserve University Center for Urban Poverty and Social Change, 1992.

Herman, J., Morris, L., and Fitz-Gibbon, C. *Evaluator's Handbook.* Newbury Park, Calif.: Sage, 1989.

Kagan, S., Golub, S., Goffin, S., and Pritchard, E. *Toward Systemic Reform: Service Integration for Young Children and Their Families.* Falls Church, Va.: National Center for Service Integration, 1995.

Kahn, A., and Kamerman, S. *Integrating Services Integration: An Overview of Initiatives, Issues and Possibilities.* New York: National Center for Children in Poverty, 1992.

Knapp, M. "How Shall We Evaluate Comprehensive, Collaborative Services for Children and Families?" *Educational Researcher,* 1995, 24 (4), 5–16.

Ooms, T. "Data Integration and Evaluation: Essential Components of Family-Centered Systems Reform." Washington, D.C.: Family Impact Seminars, 1993.

Reichardt, C. S., and Cook, T. D. "Beyond Qualitative Versus Quantitative Methods." In T. D. Cook and C. S. Reichardt (eds.), *Qualitative and Quantitative Methods in Evaluation Research.* Newbury Park, Calif.: Sage, 1979.

Reichardt, C. S., and Rallis, S. F. (eds.). *The Qualitative-Quantitative Debate: New Perspectives.* New Directions for Program Evaluation, no. 61. San Francisco: Jossey-Bass, 1994.

Young, N., Gardner, S., Coley, S., Schorr, L., and Bruner, C. *Making a Difference: Moving to Outcome-Based Accountability for Comprehensive Service Reforms.* Falls Church, Va.: National Center for Service Integration, 1994.

DONNA M. GARNETT *is executive director of the Center for Human Investment Policy at the University of Colorado's Graduate School of Public Affairs.*

MARSHA S. GOULD *is a senior research associate with the Center for Human Investment Policy.*

This chapter discusses the interaction between policy, program development, and evaluation in the reform of the human services delivery system with specific focus on the evaluation challenges and approaches to them.

Implications for the Future of Service Delivery System Reform

William A. Morrill

As this volume is prepared, the delivery of services and assistance to individuals, families, and communities across the United States is in the process of change—potentially large-scale and fundamental change—from two different directions. On one hand, the past five to ten years have seen a growing quantity and scale of experimentation and reform, stimulated primarily at the local and state levels with increasing cooperation and initiatives at the federal level. On the other hand, the recent, sharp change in the composition of the Congress has led to a redefinition of the federal role, a reduction in the level of federal resources, and devolution of federal responsibility. These two forces for change—the second more prominent, but not necessarily more important in the long run—form a powerful context for policy, program development, and evaluation of innovations and reform of the delivery system.

This volume has sought to provide definition, description, and analysis of the experimentation and reform, with a specific focus on the challenges to the evaluation of such activity and lessons learned. Here, we want both to discuss the interaction among policy, program development, and evaluation in the reform of the delivery system and to summarize the challenges we now face or may face in the future. Such an effort must immediately begin to grapple with a frustration affecting reformers and analysts alike: finding language and concepts that adequately convey understanding of what is intended and what is occurring. It is perhaps comforting to observe that the language and conceptual difficulties may arise from the possibility that something new and different is underway.

Purposes, Motivations, and Definitions

It is common enough to start a discussion on evaluation with abstract definitions from which the empirical evidence can be examined. Given the yeasty and youthful nature of the latest round of experimentation in delivery system reform, it seems useful instead to start with a description of the central themes or purposes of the reforms, as seen from a policy or managerial perspective.

The National Center for Service Integration has been among the entities and observers of the active innovation and reform efforts, along with other scholars and organizations. From these efforts, numerous taxonomies are used. In simple terms, however, four policy objectives in varying combinations emerge as the dominant themes, described here not necessarily in order of importance or emphasis.

First, the reformers seek to shift the focus of the delivery system from activities undertaken or services provided to results achieved for the intended beneficiaries. Said another way, outcome accountability is to be substituted for process measures. This objective is commonly accompanied by substantial attention within the complex institutional collaborations that undertake the reforms to the development of a shared vision of the common goals. Most serious and comprehensive reforms consider outcome-oriented performance measures and a well-articulated, shared vision, both developed bottom-up to be crucial to improved services and assistance. Despite a host of problems associated with the selection and implementation of outcome measures (as observed throughout this volume), this difficult objective is common to the most ambitious reforms.

A second central theme involves devolving authority for operational decision making concerning the scope and intensity of services provided down the intergovernmental and individual agency hierarchies directly to the recipients. Usually, this objective is pursued explicitly within the framework of civil rights protection. This theme is consistently present whether the delivery level is the field office of a large state agency, a local government entity, a community-based organization, or, most often, a collaboration with a rich array of public, nonprofit, and private organizations. This theme is often coupled with the first objective—at least conceptually—so that more local flexibility is granted in return for outcome accountability.

A third central theme in current reforms focuses on making the helping organizations and institutions—the schools, health providers, social service agencies, justice organizations, and the professionals they employ—function together in a more integrated fashion, often in formal collaborations with new governance structures. Although the collaborations may involve several or many institutions, the clear purpose is to drive beyond interagency conversation toward changes in front-line practice, serious trusting relationships across professional disciplines, efficient and user-friendly interaction between the helpers and the helped through integrated case management, and the sharing of resources across narrow program categories. Comprehensiveness in the services is a valued characteristic, with a heavy emphasis on low-cost prevention over high-cost remediation. Individual initiatives and reforms vary widely in how far they proceed (see Konrad, this volume), but this theme remains central to most serious reform. So far, this round of delivery system reform has not revived the super-department consolidations tried in the 1970s, but concentrated instead on stronger integration of the delivery system at the operating level.

The fourth theme is to adjust the relationship between the service providers and those who are helped, giving the latter more say in what help is provided and a larger responsibility in the desired outcome. This theme is reflected through various mechanisms and with varying intensity, but almost always appears in some form. At root, it is an effort to move away from a strictly hierarchical relationship between professional and client (teacher and student) toward a partnership or contract between the helper and the helped in which each party has important roles and responsibilities.

Although these objectives may be articulated in different language, number, and content, they constitute a reasonable description of what many policy makers and program managers explicitly or implicitly intend to achieve as a central part of the most ambitious and comprehensive innovations and reforms now under way. They represent a postulation of the theory of change underlying the major initiatives (Weiss, 1995), albeit a somewhat general one. Whether precisely or comprehensively stated or not, it is self-evident that the implementation of these four objectives to their logical extension represents a profound adjustment in the existing delivery system. Beyond some stunning microexperimentation, the adjustment of the system is extraordinarily difficult even on a relatively modest scale (Nelson, 1995). Furthermore, unlike the 1970s, when a similar reform effort was attempted with discretionary federal funds, today, relatively little discretionary public funding exists for such purposes.

The widespread initiatives at both state and local levels thus raise the question of why policy makers and program managers are making the enormous effort required. Not only are many initiatives under way in some form, but the innovators represent no particular ideological niche and include providers, consumers, and policy makers. Though somewhat speculative, the motivation for the reform objectives appears complex and multifaceted. One clear common thread is the conviction and the evidence that the present delivery system is producing unsatisfactory results for too large a fraction of the population at too high a societal and public-sector cost. Because the reform objectives are being sought on an increasingly larger scale in a context where the effectiveness of the reform objectives is long on conviction and short on evidence, it is reasonable to note that the inadequacies of the present delivery system seem to be keenly felt.

Beyond this common thread, motivations move along different paths. Some believe that the present structure might work given more resources, but more resources are unlikely; others believe that no level of additional resources would cure a system in need of substantial reform. This latter group and others see the reform objectives as a route to more effective services, which, if demonstrably successful, could lead to increased public confidence in the programs and more resources, if required. Some in this group believe that the reforms will produce efficiencies as well as improved effectiveness, thus leaving open the questions of whether or how many additional resources will be needed until there is more experience with the reforms.

Even with these diverging threads, there is a reasonable consensus that sees the existing delivery system as inadequate to the task and the reform objectives as the route to more effective services and assistance—potentially less costly on a unit basis, but with differing views on their aggregate budget implications. This common core is unsettled by the proposals and actions of the new congressional majority, in which aggregate budget cutting is a much more explicit and central motivation and is coupled with the reform motivations through block grant legislative proposals. Though intrinsically separable matters and not central issues in this chapter, heavy federal budget cutting and the coupling of such reductions with some of the reform objectives seem likely to both complicate the handling of the added transitional costs associated with implementation of reforms and weaken whatever motivational consensus exists for reform objectives.

With a set of underlying motivations and a group of central themes or objectives from a policy and program perspective, it is appropriate briefly to revisit the definitional issue en route to a discussion of the interactions between policy, program development, and evaluation now and in the future for delivery system reform. As noted earlier, adequate language is a problem: Are the objects of the delivery system's attention children, families, or communities? Does relabeling the entire enterprise provide a broader basis for examining delivery system reform?

In this volume, the term *services integration* has been selected to describe the current movement. Current definitions of services integration are appropriately broad and encompass the range of policy objectives and central themes described here (Konrad, this volume; Kagan and Neville, 1993). For some, services integration carries a more structural perspective and a budget-cutting connotation associated, appropriately or not, with the 1970s. Other terms with slightly different meanings but largely overlapping content have emerged. Comprehensive services is one. *Reform of the delivery system,* used more often in this chapter to avoid any inappropriate historic baggage associated with services integration, is another common descriptor. Consistency of language and precision in meaning are unquestionably long-term objectives, but for a field still inchoate, it is appropriate to concentrate on the overlapping meanings rather than the marginal distinctions. Furthermore, it is the central themes and objectives that are important to the interaction among policy, practice, and evaluation. With a construct of what the policy makers and program managers intend to accomplish, we can then turn to evaluation challenges. What are we going to measure and how?

Inherent Evaluation Challenges

The central themes of the innovations and reforms in the service delivery system through which policy makers and program managers are seeking to improve delivery system functioning provide a useful structure for evaluation activities. Are the four themes or objectives being effectively pursued and, if so, is that pursuit leading to improved outcomes? If working only partially, in what circumstances and for what groups is it working, and why is it not working for others? For all the apparent successes, how can we be sure it is the innovation or reform that has produced the desired result, as opposed to other known or unknown and unmeasured forces and influences?

Although the policy themes provide useful structure and the questions are deceptively straightforward, concepts and practices embedded in these same themes are at odds in important ways with conventional evaluation concepts and practices. In general, evaluation practice seeks to isolate, stabilize, and simplify, whereas the central themes in delivery system reform seek to integrate, modify, and make complex. These conflicts occur across a series of important evaluation issues that must be described followed by discussion of approaches to resolution.

In addition to the tension between policy and evaluation objectives, there are further issues within the evaluation community and among disciplines as to what constitutes an appropriate standard of evidence for evaluation findings. The posture taken in this chapter is that the most interesting and ambitious delivery system reform initiatives push to the limits the capability of all of the existing evaluation tools across the disciplines, and thus the central challenge is to make judicious use of all tools at our disposal, importantly recognizing the stage to which the reform itself has progressed. The reforms are at an early stage of development. There is as yet no consensus or evidence about which package of services and assistance, in what configuration, with what targeting priorities, and at what scale to impact a significant area (such as a city) is an appropriate model. It has not yet been tried, although efforts to get to such experimentation are beginning. Under this set of circumstances, an effort to mount the definitive impact evaluation would not only be difficult, it probably would not even be a productive use of the substantial funds needed to conduct it. This judgment, shared by other evaluators, is not to suggest that in the long run experimental impact evaluations have no place in an evaluation strategy (Hollister and Hill, 1995; Knapp, 1995).

The professional debates about standards of evidence and the desirability of rigorous impact analyses for researchers and policy makers alike should not cloud the fact that it is not important to know everything in order to learn something useful at this point in the development of the reform of the delivery systems. Contributions from ethnography, case studies, process and cost analyses, program and community indicators, and (where and when plausible) experimental and quasi-experimental evaluations will all be needed as the reforms and their assessments mature. Each alone and, more importantly, all in concert can add incrementally to our knowledge about the value of the initiatives. A rigorous impact evaluation design may be needed to attribute with certainty the causalities of observed results, but such an evaluation is not required to determine whether the primary mechanisms of the reforms and innovations are being executed, and whether better or worse outcomes are occurring.

With this perspective, we can now turn to some of the specific challenges to evaluation posed by the delivery system reforms. The first two of these challenges arise from the complexity and scope of the reforms in their pursuit of functional comprehensiveness and collaborative action.

Unit of Analysis Problem. In whose behavior or outcomes are we interested when evaluating the reforms of the delivery system? Conventional evaluation methodology would drive us toward simplification—usually to a single unit of analysis and, most often, to the individual. That answer does not suffice for the innovative, comprehensive initiatives, for such an approach leaves out important and intended results of the initiative. At a minimum, the comprehensive initiative is interested in the effects on the individual, the family, and the community (Hollister and Hill, 1995). The reforms are predicated on interactive effects among these three units, and therefore the evaluation must examine the impact on all three, which adds significantly to the evaluation's scope and complexity.

Though somewhat different in character than the ultimate consumers or beneficiaries of the services and assistance, an argument can also be made that the delivery system organizations are a critical unit of analysis. The reform is predicated on the notion that how those organizations behave and perform is a vital instrumentality to the outcomes for consumers; hence, system reform to achieve better outcomes requires thorough understanding of effective institutional structure and behavior. This increment to the units of analysis further complicates the evaluation process, but its inclusion is compelling. One needs only to recall some of the impact evaluations of the late 1960s, which reported negligible effects on individuals when the real story was negligible interventions from the delivery system.

Outcome Issues and the Profusion of Variables. The complexity and scope of comprehensive delivery system reforms also create problems in the definition and selection of both outcomes and independent variables. What outcomes are appropriate to measure? Which independent variables should be included? Again, evaluation methodology drives in the direction of fewer and simpler, and the reforms are pushing in the other direction. The issues concerning outcomes and variables take several different forms.

The first dimension affecting both outcomes and variables is the profusion problem. Many outcomes are of interest, and many variables are of potential importance in explaining observed outcomes (Knapp, 1995). Because of the inherent complexity and the early stage of system reform development, there seems to be no way to avoid this problem; but it does raise the potential for false starts, muddling through, and a substantial reporting overload on innovation sites and their management information systems (MIS). This latter potential issue, if not carefully managed, could mean weakened data quality from program management information systems that are critical to evaluation work at this stage of development (Marzke, 1994). Muddling through may be the only available strategy. Such a strategy should put a premium on close interaction within the concerned evaluation community and between that community and the innovators and reformers, so that learning and insight are quickly shared.

A second dimension of the outcomes issue lies in the strategy for their selection and definition, in which it is important to avoid two difficulties. The first difficulty is the potential confusion between goals and outcome expectations. It is easy enough to envision the end stage goal of a reformed delivery system—for example, happy, functioning, and productive families in a thriving community—and quite another matter to set that goal as an outcome expectation for a modest service integration innovation of school-based services in its early stages. The longer-term goals are important, but not when translated into unrealistic short-term outcome measures that set excessive expectations that can frustrate innovators and public support. Intermediate outcome measures that can reflect steady progress toward longer-term goals are needed to fuel the necessary outcome accountability objective without unrealistic overpromising. The second difficulty is the tempting retreat to process or activity measures when outcome measures are hard to define, particularly in the intermediate stage of development. Simply stated, the temptation should be avoided.

A final dimension of the outcomes issue is also related to the strategy for selection. It concerns what basis should be used in selecting a manageable set of variables. As suggested earlier, one clearly wants to take account in the selection of the central themes of the reform. In addition, however, another approach for reducing the numerous possibilities to more manageable and realistic numbers is to focus on measurable outcomes with clear connection to community goals that are collectible on at least an annual basis (Bruner, 1995).

Beyond the challenges to evaluation presented by the unit of analysis and the outcome and independent-variable issues, there are two additional challenges posed for evaluation. They deal with how evaluation is used to identify best practices and learn from past experiences, and how those lessons can be used to adopt successful components of service delivery reform efforts or to make improvements when explicating models in different projects or across sites.

Replication and Stable Intervention Issues. Evaluation practice strongly prefers well-defined and stable interventions so that evaluation findings can be clearly used in transferring best practices to new sites. Well-defined and stable interventions are also important to impact evaluations where observations are pooled across sites to assess outcomes for consumers. These practices are clearly challenged by the stage and objectives of the reform movement. The interventions are highly varied and dynamic because the reform is at a developmental stage. Complicating this, one of the central themes involves bottom-up consensus in the definition of the intervention, thus making variability and dynamic change a virtue. This reality seems likely to complicate cross-site evaluations, meta-analyses, and model-building for the foreseeable future (Knapp, 1995).

Replication and Feedback Issues. Because these programs are evolutionary in their development, it is important to pay attention to potential effects of the evaluation on the program. The issue here is whether that influence is inappropriate. In circumstances where the project or program is being evaluated in order to assess the desirability of its replication in its tested form, then feedback is clearly a problem for replication elsewhere, because it could alter the intervention.

Those circumstances, however, do not apply to the current stage of development of delivery system reform. The precise character of the reforms are not set, but are in development. Thus the feedback loops in the developmental stage are desirable rather than adverse. Innovators, technical assistance providers, and evaluators in the developmental stage should be seen more as partners than independent operators or adversaries. Further, even at later stages, the losses of the purity of replication findings may be more than offset by the improved quality of the program data from the MIS for evaluation purposes; this can occur from constructive and respectful interaction between program operators and evaluators.

The insistence on models for various purposes in the reform of the delivery system as a general matter is premature. Too little is known about the most effective groupings of services, governance structures, operational processes, practice approaches and other important features to establish clear, successful models. Significant variation and experimentation are appropriate and needed to uncover effective combinations and best practice. This point, however, is not to say that careful conceptualization, thorough documentation, and thoughtful analysis are inappropriate for each initiative; indeed, they are critical.

The two evaluation challenges associated with replication issues are joined by a major issue associated with impact evaluations. These evaluations, designed to establish definitive outcomes associated with particular interventions, present serious problems in their application to comprehensive systems reform that are not yet resolved.

Comparison Groups and the Counterfactual. The purpose of serious impact evaluation is to sort out observed results attributable to a deliberate intervention, as opposed to what would have happened anyway in the absence of the intervention, known as the counterfactual. The randomized experiment is the best-known method for achieving this result, because it deals effectively not only with measured variables but with unmeasured and potentially important variables as well. All other techniques, although often used, produce less certain results in attributing causalities.

The delivery system reform initiatives defy randomized experimentation. At the individual or family level, randomization is impractical; although randomization at the community level is an interesting notion, it is certainly an expensive one. Thus, impact evaluations of delivery system reforms at least in the short run seem doomed to less certain methods of assessing impact (Hollister and Hill, 1995).

Alternative approaches to impact evaluations can move in two different directions. One direction would undertake or make use of rigorous impact evaluations with random assignment or matched control groups for component elements of the delivery system reform, the results of which could be incorporated into the reform design (Knapp, 1995). If, for example, a particularly effective approach to community health and wellness was uncovered and validated in a rigorous impact evaluation, it could be integrated with some assurance that it would contribute positively to the overall reform effectiveness.

The second choice would be to make judicious use of other, less certain evaluation techniques such as pre- and post-analyses or the dose-response techniques. In the first place, one cannot be certain, given the dynamic forces in large communities, whether all forces that act on that community are sufficiently understood to isolate a cause-and-effect relationship between the reforms undertaken and the outcomes measured. Indeed, it is more likely that something is not well-understood. Nonetheless, if measured outcomes are improving at reasonable costs, the policy community may be happy to live with some uncertainty about causalities. It is only in the face of no improvement or, worse, deterioration in measured outcomes that the policy community may and perhaps should become dissatisfied with the reforms.

Dose-response techniques might involve deliberate variation of component elements within a reform community and the outcomes assessed. For example, the intensity of psychosocial services for troubled adolescents might be sharply varied to assess behavioral impacts and cost-effectiveness at some risk to the certainty of the findings because of unobserved variables, even after controlling for observed differences in socioeconomic status. Findings might, nonetheless, provide some clues to the usefulness of the sources.

Although these second choices are less certain and need to be applied with care, they can prove helpful in conjunction with other techniques to assess the progress and effectiveness of the experimentation now under way in the reform of the delivery system.

Approaches for the Period Ahead

The central themes of the reform of the delivery system from a policy perspective produce a useful framework and starting point for an incremental and continuing evaluation effort of the reforms, and set the stage for an important set of interactions among concerned policy makers, program managers, technical assistance providers, and evaluators. Although evaluators must apply the full range of evaluation techniques, some methodologies and practices are significantly challenged and are of limited utility, at least in the short run. Experience to date suggests that evaluations of the most ambitious, comprehensive, and interesting initiatives in delivery system reform, as well as the implementation of the reforms themselves, are very difficult (Connell, 1995; Nelson, 1995; Center for the Study of Social Policy, 1995). These points lead to consideration of what actions and what work should be given emphasis in the period ahead. Although no topic of importance should go unattended, certain work or actions should be given high priority.

Conceptualization. As suggested here, conceptualization or theory-based evaluations of the reforms should be pursued, refined, and detailed as an iterative structuring of evaluations (Weiss, 1995). The detailing should be closely aligned with community objectives (Bruner, 1995). Empirical work is of great importance, but collection of experience without a conceptual framework is likely to be more confusing than helpful.

Descriptive Analysis and Documentation. Too many interesting initiatives have been launched with no evaluation or documentation of any kind. The deficiency is improving, but the loss of valuable lessons is regrettable. Even if measuring consumer outcomes is beyond available resources, no serious delivery system reform should be launched without a careful and ongoing descriptive analysis and documentation component. It should include a conceptual framework, startup and continuing operation history inclusive of barriers faced and problems resolved, services and assistance provided, governance adopted, processes revised, training undertaken, professional practices adjusted, relationships with consumers transformed, and outcomes tracked with results.

Information Systems. No comprehensive system reform is likely to persist without a supportive information system. That work should be initiated early with careful attention to the burden it imposes on program operations and the support it provides to front-line workers. Without such attention, whatever other data it contains is likely to be of limited quality. With such attention, however, the information system is likely to be a critical component of an effective evaluation strategy, particularly in this developmental stage.

Networking. Learning in the developmental stage of the reform is not only important, but is usually welcome among the innovators who have countless problems to resolve and appreciate assistance. Indeed, lessons may be more cheerfully absorbed at this stage before large-scale changes have been set in place. This suggests the desirability of substantial and continuing networking not only among evaluators, but across policy makers, program managers, technical assistance providers, and evaluators. Some of this activity is already under way, but it can be strengthened and deepened.

Cost Analyses, Outcomes, and Indicators. Together with the work on descriptive analysis, continuing work is needed on assessing the costs of the reformed system, leading to cost comparisons with the present system. This exceedingly difficult work will be of great importance in program monitoring in the meantime, while satisfactory frameworks for cost-effectiveness or cost-benefit analysis can be established. Similarly, continuing work on outcomes and indicators for all units of analysis both for the short run and the long run is of high priority.

Comparative Analyses. This area of evaluation work raises some of the most troublesome issues with the least apparent resolution. Rigorous impact evaluations falter on the difficulties of structuring high-confidence comparison groups. Even if these problems can be overcome, direct measurement of all but aggregate impacts with comprehensive reforms seems beyond reach; component impact will need to be measured separately. Alternative and creative approaches to comparative analyses should also constitute a high-priority endeavor.

As a final observation about the period ahead, the sharp change in Congress noted at the outset may introduce still other adjustments in the appropriate strategy. Federal financial resources will clearly be smaller, and federal involvement in the tradeoff between operational flexibility and outcome accountability may also wane and become more importantly a state problem. Fewer federal resources may discourage reform innovation by limiting transitional funds often important in new processes. However, none of the issues that have fueled the current reform movement will have changed, and all of the issues identified herein will remain to be attacked.

References

Bruner, C. "A Framework for Developing and Holding Comprehensive Reform Efforts Accountable for Improving Child Outcomes." Working paper. Des Moines, Iowa: Child and Family Policy Center, June 1995.

Center for the Study of Social Policy. *Building New Futures for At-Risk Youth: Findings from a Five-Year Multi-Site Evaluation.* Washington, D.C.: Center for the Study of Social Policy, 1995.

Connell, J. P., Kubisch, A. C., Schorr, L. B., and Weiss, C. H. (eds.). *New Approaches to Evaluating Community Initiatives.* Washington, D.C.: Aspen Institute, 1995.

Hollister, R. G., and Hill, J. "Problems in the Evaluation of Community-Wide Initiatives." In J. P. Connell, A. C. Kubisch, L. B. Schorr, and C. H. Weiss (eds.), *New Approaches to Evaluating Community Initiatives.* Washington, D.C.: Aspen Institute, 1995.

Kagan, S. L., and Neville, P. R. *Integrating Services for Children and Families: Understanding the Past to Shape the Future.* New Haven, Conn.: Yale University Press, 1993.

Knapp, M. S. "How Shall We Study Comprehensive, Collaborative Services for Children and Families?" *Educational Researcher,* 1995, 24 (4), 5–16.

Marzke, C., Both, D., and Focht, J. *Information Systems to Support Comprehensive Human Service Delivery: Emerging Approaches, Issues, and Opportunities.* Des Moines, Iowa: National Center for Service Integration, 1994.

Nelson, D. W. *The Path of Most Resistance: Reflections on Lessons Learned from New Futures.* Baltimore, Md.: Annie E. Casey Foundation, 1995.

Weiss, C. H. "Nothing as Practical as Good Theory: Exploring Theory-Based Evaluation for Comprehensive Community Initiatives for Children and Families." In J. P. Connell, A. C. Kubisch, L. P. Schorr, and C. H. Weiss (eds.), *New Approaches to Evaluating Community Initiatives.* Washington, D.C.: Aspen Institute, 1995.

WILLIAM A. MORRILL is chair of Mathtech, Inc., and director of the National Center for Service Integration.

INDEX

Adler, L., 52
Administration for Children, Youth, and Families, 48
American Educational Research Association, 8
American Evaluation Association (AEA), 1
Amos, K. J., 36, 48
Annie E. Casey Foundation, 28
Aronson, J. Z., 8, 11, 15
Asayesh, G., 8
Automated information systems: child and family services and, 31; human services delivery reform evaluation and, 94; measures of, 17; services integration initiatives and, 16–17. *See also* Data management; Management information systems (MIS)

Bazron, B., 46
Blank, J., 8
Both, D., 23, 31, 91
Boyd, W. L., 8, 9, 23, 25, 27
Brewer, E. J., 36
Bronheim, D., 36, 48
Bruner, C., 5, 25, 31, 91, 94

California Department of Education, 52, 55, 56
California Partnership for School-Linked Services, 52–53
California school-based services initiatives, 51–66. *See also* Healthy Start program
Casanova, U., 26
Castco, G., 36
Center for the Study of Social Policy, 28, 94
Chackerian, R., 6, 11, 12
Chen, H-T., 20
Child and family services: conceptual research on, 27; data management and, 31; deficit model of, 26; Family Support and Preservation Programs, 48; 4C program, 7; guidelines for, 73; higher-level integration of, 13, 23, 71; infant mortality reduction and, 36–37; MCHB, 36; National Center for Clinical Infant programs, 48; New Futures initiative, 28; outcomes for, 23–24; school-based

systems for, 52; social conditions or position and, 26. *See also* Family Centers Initiative; Human services; State Efforts in Early Childhood (SEEC) Management Team
Children's Action Alliance, 12, 16
Chimerine, C. B., 23
CHSPDS. *See* Comprenehsive Human Services Planning and Delivery Systems (CHSPDS)
Chynoweth, J., 53, 54
CISS. *See* Community Integrated Services Systems (CISS)
Cohen, E., 12, 17, 72
Colorado Children's Campaign, 74
Colorado, state-level integrated services initiatives in, 69–84. *See also* Family Centers Initiative; State Efforts in Early Childhood (SEEC) Management Team
Commission on Families and Children (Colo.), 70–71, 76
Communication: level of integration and, 9; service delivery model and, 14
Communities Can, 48
Community: client- and program-centered services integration in, 69–70; state-initiated services integration and, 69
Community Coordinated Child Care (4C), 7
Community Integrated Services Systems (CISS): administrative levels and policy development relationship, 43; client entry, 44; cross-project study of, 38; descriptive study of, 38; geography, 43; infant mortality and maternal health goals of, 36–37, 41; intervention focus of, 44; MCHB interest in, 37–39; objectives of, 37; origins of, 36–37; policy implications and analysis of, 38–39; population of, 43; principles of, 37, 46; projects relationship framework of, 41–42; proposed studies of, 38–39; RFPs for, 37–38; services offered by, 44; strategies for, 43–44; time constraints and, 45; training needs and, 45
Community Integrated Services Systems (CISS) projects, evaluation: background variables and, 41–42; community ecology and, 48; construct measures and, 47;

97

Community Integrated Services Systems (CISS) (continued)
cross-site, 42–46; descriptive results, 42–44; framework, 41–42; goal definition and relevance and, 47; goal evaluability and, 47; individual project vs. cross-site, 39–41; intended target population and, 47–48; key process and outcome variables measures, 45–46; lessons from, 46–48; methods, 42; outcome measures of, 39–40; outcomes of, 39–40, 42; plan (example 1), 40; plan (example 2), 40–41; program components and, 42; project planning and, 47; rating scales and, 46; system development issues and, 45; telephone interview results, 44–45
Comprehensive Human Services Planning and Delivery Systems (CHSPDS), 7
Connell, J. P., 94
Coulton, C., 69, 76
Counterfactual, 92
Cronbach, L. J., 22
Cross, T., 46
Crowson, R. L., 8, 9, 23, 25, 27

Data management: automated information systems and, 17; services delivery reform and, 90–91; services integration evaluation and, 30–31; services integration initiatives and, 16–17. See also Automated information systems; Management information systems (MIS)
Deficit Reduction Act of 1984, 7
Dennis, K., 46
Department of Health and Human Services (HHS), 6, 7, 37
Dryfoos, J., 52
Dunst, C. J., 39
Dym, B., 26, 27

Evaluation: characteristics of rigorous, 53; coaching and, 61–62; conceptualization and design of, 38; definitions of, 22; expectations about, 3; federal program, 35–36; formative vs. summative, 22; process vs. impact, 22; program effectiveness and implementation and, 38; self, 72, 80–81; skepticism and, 27–28; stable intervention issues and, 91–92; stakeholders and, 22. See also Community Integrated Services Systems (CISS) projects, evaluation; Family Centers Initiative, evaluation; Human services delivery reform, evaluation; Services integration evaluation; Services integration evaluation, state-level; State Efforts in Early Childhood (SEEC) Management Team, evaluation
Evaluators: conceptual frameworks of, 26; dependent variables and, 24; independent variables and, 24; language gap and, 22–23; outcomes questions of, 25; partnerships of, 28; services integration challenges for, 3, 5, 21; social intervention problems and, 25–26
Evans, J. E., 46
Exemplary and typical practice studies, 30

Factor-analytic studies, 31
Family Centers Initiative: collaborative and integrative approach of, 77; Colorado's Strategic Plan and, 70–71; Commission on Families and Children and, 70–71, 76; components of, 76–77, 79; crisis intervention assistance and, 79; demographics of, 77; family-friendly activities of, 80; family support of, 82; first wave of, 76–77; funding and, 77, 80–81; goals of, 70, 76; implementation phase of, 81; integration barriers and, 81–82; origin of, 70–71, 76; planning strategies of, 81; principles of, 76
Family Centers Initiative, evaluation: child and family outcomes of, 82–83; conclusions of, 81–82; design of, 77; formative nature of, 72; in-depth interviews and, 78–79; issues for, 71–72; multidimensional nature of, 71–72; observations and, 79–80; parent-focus groups and, 79; qualitative approach to, 72–73; quantitative approach to, 72; rating assessment and, 78–79; self-evaluations and, 80–81; services integration goals and, 71; systemic outcomes of, 72
Family Impact Seminar, 8, 31
Family services. See Child and family services
Family Support and Preservation Programs, 48
Farrow, F., 15
Federal government: CHSPDS projects, 7; CISS projects evaluation by, 35–48; evaluation by, 35–36; 4C program, 7; HEW initiatives, 6–7; HHS initiatives,

7–8; OEO programs, 35; partnerships with private foundations, 8; services integration initiatives in, 6–8; shifting role of, 8; SIPPs, 7; SITO projects, 7
Financing strategies, 16
Fitz-Gibbon, C., 72
Focht, J., 91
4C. See Community Coordinated Child Care (4Ċ)
Freeman, H. E., 38
Frumkin, M. L., 6, 11, 12

Gardner, S., 52
General Accounting Office, 6, 25, 51, 52
Goffin, S. G., 6, 7
Golan, S., 63
Golden, O., 23, 28
Golub, S. A., 6, 7
Gomby, D. S., 31
Governance models, 14
Government. See Federal government; Service integration evaluation, state-level; State government
Greene, J. G., 22, 26, 31
Group-comparative studies, 31–32
Guilfoyle, K., 26
Guthrie, G. P., 8, 11, 15
Guthrie, L. F., 8, 11, 15

Halpern, R., 5
Health services: infant mortality and, 36–37; maternal care, 36–37. See also Community Integrated Services Systems (CISS); Department of Health and Human Services (HHS); Maternal and Child Health Bureau (MCHB)
Healthy Kids, Healthy California, 54
Healthy Start program: broad scope of, 57; California Partnership for School-Linked Services and, 52–53; case management in, 56; expectations of, 56–57; family focus of, 56; financing of, 53; goal of, 54; grant awards of, 54; individual intervention experiences in, 56; intervention variation in, 55; limited funding of, 57; multiple stakeholders in, 56–57; multisite and multidimensionality of, 54; origins of, 52; other related policy initiatives and, 54–55; population differences in, 55–56; public-private partnerships and, 52–53; service activities of, 60–61; site evaluation experience in, 57; systemic change and, 54

Healthy Start program evaluation: approach of, 57–63; challenges of, 53–57; collaboration and, 58; compliance with, 57; conceptual framework of, 58–59; confidentiality and, 60–61; core vs. site-specific measures of, 60; design of, 58, 60; early outcomes of, 63–65; evaluation coaching and, 61–62; evaluator selection for, 53; fiscal constraints and, 57; future directions for, 64–65; identification systems and, 61; mandate for, 53; outcome measures of, 60; randomized trial design and, 54; reports on, 62–63; service activity measures of, 60; site support and, 61–62
Healthy Start Support Services for Children Act, 52
Henderson, J., 53, 54
Herman, J., 72
HHS. See Department of Health and Human Services (HHS)
Hill, J., 89, 90
Hollister, R. G., 89, 90
Human services: cost reduction of, 1; federal involvement in, 85; fragmentation of, 1; philosophical reorientation of, 1; social position and, 26. See Child and family services; Health services
Human services delivery: change in, 85; inadequacy of, 6, 13; integration goals for, 71; local-global shift in, 5; organization-centered restructuring of, 70. See also Service delivery model
Human services delivery reform: activity vs. results focus of, 86; collaborative and integrative focus of, 86; comprehensive focus of, 86–87; definition of, 88; difficulty of, 87; federal role in, 85; funding and, 87; local flexibilty and, 86; local and state impetus for, 85; motivations for, 87–88; outcome accountability and, 86; partnership focus of, 87; policy objectives of, 86–87; prevention and remediation focus of, 87; service provider focus of, 87; shift of authority to recipients in, 86; system inadequacy and, 88
Human services delivery reform, evaluation: bottom-up consensus and, 92; challenges for, 89–93; comparative analyses and, 95; comparison groups and, 92–93; complexity of, 90, 94; concepualization and, 95; cost analyses and, 94; counterfactual and, 92; descriptive

Human services delivery reform (*continued*) analysis and documentation and, 94; dose-response techniques and, 93; future approaches to, 93–95; goals vs. outcome expectations and, 91; impact analyses and, 89–90, 92; information systems and, 94; networking and, 95; organizational behavior and, 90; outcomes and indicators and, 94; outcomes issues and, 90–91; policy objectives and, 89; pre- and post-analyses and, 93; randomized experimentation and, 92; replication and feedback issues and, 92; replication and stable intervention issues and, 91–92; standard of evidence and, 89; theory-building and, 94; unit-of-analysis problem and, 90; variables issues and, 90–91

Human services integration. *See* Services integration (SI)

Hurchins, V., 36

IDEA. *See* Individuals with Disabilities Education Act (IDEA)

Imershein, A. W., 6, 11, 12

Impact analyses, 89–90, 92

Individual participation and change studies, 29

Individuals with Disabilities Education Act (IDEA), 48

Integration. *See* Services integration (SI)

Invitational Working Conference on Comprehensive School-Linked Services for Children and Families, 8

Isaacs, M., 46

Kagan, S. L., 6, 7, 23, 24, 69, 70, 71, 88

Kahn, A. J., 12, 46, 69

Kamerman, S. B., 12, 46, 69

Kane, H., 37, 38, 42, 44, 46

Keefe, M. L., 36, 48

Kelley, F., 63

Keough, B. K., 46

Knapp, M. S., 9, 26, 28, 46, 71, 72, 89, 90, 92, 93

Koop, C. E., 36

Kubisch, A. C., 94

Kusserow, R. P., 6, 12

Labin, S. M., 18

Lam, K. K., 37, 38, 42, 44, 46

Lam, W.J.J., 36, 46

Larson, C. S., 31, 52

Lipman, P., 23

Low-Income Opportunity Advisory Board, 8

McPherson, M., 36

Magrab, P. R., 36

Management information systems (MIS), 91. *See also* Automated information systems; Data management

Marks, E. L., 23

Martin, P. Y., 6, 11, 12

Marzke, C., 91

Maternal and Child Health Bureau (MCHB): block grant program of, 36; CISS projects of, 36–48; community services commitment of, 36; infant mortality and maternal health goals of, 36–37, 41; interest in CISS evaluation by, 37–39

Mawhinney, H., 27

MCHB. *See* Maternal and Child Health Bureau (MCHB)

Melaville, A. I., 8

Meta-analytic studies, 31

Mitchell, D. E., 27, 66

Morgan, C. C., 36, 48

Morrill, W. A., 14, 23

Morris, L., 72

National Center for Children in Poverty, 6

National Center for Clinical Infant programs, 48

National Center for Service Integration, 6

Nelson, D. W., 87, 94

Nelville, P. R., 88

New Futures initiative, 28

OEO. *See* Office of Economic Opportunity (OEO)

Office of Economic Opportunity (OEO), 35

Office of Human Development Services, 7

O'Looney, J., 46

Ooms, T., 12, 15, 17, 72

Opening Doors Project, 48

Outcomes: child and family, 24, 71, 73, 82–83; complexity of, 25; definition of, 91; dependent variables and, 24–25; goals and, 91; human services delivery reform and, 94; inappropriate program combination and negative, 18; individual- and family-level, 17; individual and group, 24–25; measurement of, 17; new service system, 17; profusion of, 90–91; program, 18; program vs. integration, 17–18; program-specific indicators and, 18; questions on, 17–18; selection strategy for, 91; services integration initiatives and, 16; stakeholders and, 23; synergistic, 17; system, 25

Partnerships: cost-effectiveness of, 18; evaluator-staff, 28; focus on, in services reform, 87; helper-helpee, 87; members of SI, 12; power sharing and, 23–24; public-private, 8, 52; school-community, 8; services integration evaluation and, 18; services integration initiatives and, 12, 52. See also California Partnership for School-Linked Services
Patton, M. Q., 22, 26
Philliber Research Associates, 23, 51
Placier, L., 26
Point-of-service delivery studies, 29
Presley-Brown Interagency Children's Services Act of 1989, 54
Pritchard, E., 6, 7

Quantitative and qualitative cost analysis, 29–30

Rallis, S. F., 72
Ramey, C. T., 36
Reform. See Human services delivery reform
Reichardt, C. S., 72
Reisner, E. R., 23
Richardson, V., 26
Roberts, R. N., 36, 37, 38, 42, 46, 48
Rossi, P. H., 31, 38

Sandler, L., 11
School-linked services initiatives: California, 51–66; definition of, 51–52; description of, 51; evaluation of, 51; financing of, 53; growth of, 8, 51–52; policy making and, 52; private support for, 52; underlying philosophy of, 52. See also Healthy Start program
Schorr, L. B., 23, 24, 31, 94
Scott, B. L., 8, 11, 15
Scott, L. D., 27, 66
Scriven, M., 22
Service delivery model: case management and, 15; communications and, 14;

dimensions of, 14–15; geographic location and, 14–15; other subdimensions of, 15; service configuration and, 14–15; staff deployment and, 14; training and, 14. See also Human services delivery
Services integration (SI): approaches to, 69–70; assistance for, 8; attributes of, 46; benefits of, 6; categorical programs vs., 6, 13; challenges of, 3, 5, 21; child and family outcomes of, 71; client-centered approach to, 69-70; collaboration level of, 11; comparison populations and, 3; conceptual research on, 27; conferences on, 8; consolidation level of, 11; cooperation and coordination level of, 11; data systems and, 3; deep structure examination of, 27; definitions of, 9, 46, 88; delivery issues in, 69; developmental approach to, 3; goal of, 71; gradations of, 81–82; impetus for, 6; information and sharing level of, 9–11; instability of, 3; integration level of, 11; lessons from, 3; levels of, 9–11; local- vs. state-initiated, 69–70; mixed-methods approaches to, 4; motives for, 1; multifaceted nature of, 5; nonintegrated programs vs., 6; organization-centered approach to, 70; policy-centered approach to, 70; policy making and, 69; professional and institutional norms and, 27; program-centered approach to, 70; program theory and, 3; project politics and, 3; reinventing the wheel and, 1; self-evaluation and, 72; systemic accomplishment of, 71; variability of, 23; variables relationship framework and, 41–42. See also Human services delivery; Services integration dimensions; Services integration evaluation; Services integration initiatives
Services integration dimensions: categorization of, 23–24; financing, 15–16; goals, 13; governance and authority, 13–14; information systems and data management, 16–17; key, 12–17; licensing and contracting, 16; matrix of, 10; outcomes and accountability, 16; partners, 12; planning and budgeting, 15; program policy and legislation, 13; relative importance of, 18; service delivery model and, 14–15; services integration evaluation and, 18; stakeholders, 15; target population, 12–13; variance on, 12

Services integration evaluation: bottom-up, 28; collaborative, 28–29; Communities Can, 48; community-based programs and, 48; comparative, 27; compromise and, 23; confusion about, 32; constructively skeptical, 27–28; cost analysis and, 29–30; dangers of, 32; data management information systems analysis and, 30–31; dependent variables and, 24–25; descriptive, 27; design for, 3, 21; desirable attributes for, 26–29; difficulties of, 21–22; diverse perspectives and, 22–23; effectiveness and, 18; effects of causes and, 25–26; exemplary and typical practice and, 30; expectations and, 4; factor-analytic studies and, 31; formative vs. summative, 71; group-comparative studies and, 31–32; ideal program and, 18; independent variables and, 23–24; individual- and family-level outcomes and, 17; individual and group outcomes and, 24–25; individual participation and change profiles, 29; integrated services complexity and, 21–22; issues and questions for, 17–18, 22–26, 71–72; language gap and, 22–23; means and ends issues and, 25; measurement and, 17, 23; meta-analytic studies and, 31; multidisciplinary teams and, 22; multiple-case and point-of-service studies and, 29–30; need for appropriate, 32; new service system effects and, 17; Opening Doors Project, 48; outcomes measures and, 17–18, 25; partnerships and, 18; promising approaches to, 29–31; qualitative vs. quantitative, 72; recipients and, 23; rhetoric about, 32; self-evaluation and, 72; services integration dimensions and, 18; single-subject time-series, 30; social theory and, 23; strongly concepualized, 26–27; synergistic effects and, 17; system outcomes and, 25; useful results of, 31–32. See also Community Integrated Services Systems (CISS) projects, evaluation; Family Centers Initiative, evaluation; Healthy Start program, evaluation; Services integration evaluation, state-level; State Efforts in Early Childhood (SEEC) Management Team, evaluation

Services integration evaluation, state-level: conceptual definition and, 83; consensus approach and, 82–83; contextual issues and, 72; as dynamic process, 83; issues in, 71–72; lessons about, 83–84; process and outcome assessment and, 83; qualitative approach and, 72; quantitative approach and, 72; relevance of, 83; self-evaluations and, 72, 80–81; stakeholders in, 84; success and, 83. See also Family Centers Initiative, evaluation; Human services delivery reform, evaluation; State Efforts in Early Childhood (SEEC) Management Team, evaluation

Services integration initiatives: authority for, 13–14; child and youth, 24; CHSPDS projects, 7; CISS, 36–37; client assumptions and, 26; collaboration level and, 11; Communities Can, 48; community-based, 48; complexity and multidimensional nature of, 21; conceptual models of, 26–27; consolidation level of, 11; consumer-focused, 28; cooperation and coordination level of, 11; cost analysis of, 29–30; data management analysis and, 30–31; deficit model and, 26; definition of, 5–6; dimensions of, 11–17; dimensions and integration matrix of, 10; diverse perspectives of, 22–23; effectiveness and, 18; exemplary and typical practice and, 30; for families and children, 23; Family Support and Preservation Programs, 48; federal, 6–8; financing strategies and, 15–16; formal vs. informal decision making and, 14; formality vs. informality of, 9; 4C program, 7; goals of, 13; governance for, 14–15; government-private sector partnerships and, 8; HHS, 7; history of, 6–9; IDEA and, 48; ideal, 18; independent operation and, 9; independent variables of, 23; individual participation and change and, 29; individual and system impact of, 30; information sharing and communication level of, 9–11; information systems and, 16–17; integration levels of, 9–11; level of intensity of, 9; licensing and contracting and, 16; literature review of, 8–9; MCHB and, 36; measurement of, 17; multiple levels of, 23; New Futures, 28; in 1970s, 6–7; in 1980s, 7–8; in 1990s, 8–9; Opening Doors Project, 48; outcomes and accountability and, 16; outcomes measures and, 17–18; partnerships and, 12, 28; planning and budgeting and, 15; point-of-service delivery and, 29; power sharing and, 23–24; range of, 23; scale and scope of, 24; service delivery models for, 14–15; services redefinition and relocation and, 23; SIPPs, 7–8; SITO projects, 7; stakeholders and, 15; state, 7–8; system reform and, 23; target population of, 12–13; theory of action, 26–27; treatment mutability and, 24. *See also* Community Integrated Services Systems (CISS); Family Centers Initiative; Healthy Start program; Services integration dimensions; School-linked services initiatives; State Efforts in Early Childhood (SEEC) Management Team

Services Integration Pilot Projects (SIPPs), 7–8

Services Integration Targets of Opportunity (SITO), 7

SI. *See* Services integration (SI)

SIPPs. *See* Services Integration Pilot Projects (SIPPs)

SITO. *See* Services Integration Targets of Opportunity (SITO)

Smith, G., 23

Stakeholders: diversity of, 23; evaluation and, 22; Healthy Start program, 56–57; outcomes and, 23; services integration initiatives and, 15; state-level services integration evaluation, 84

State Efforts in Early Childhood (SEEC) Management Team: child and family guidelines of, 73; collaborative approach and, 75; Colorado's *Strategic Plan* and, 70–71, 76; comprehensive service packages and, 76; early intervention and prevention efforts and, 76; family support of, 82; funding for, 74; goals of, 70, 72; integration barriers and, 75, 82; members of, 72; origins of, 70–71; outcome indicators of, 73–74; policy-centered approach and, 70

State Efforts in Early Childhood (SEEC) Management Team, evaluation: child and family outcomes and, 82–83; conclusions of, 75–76; demographic trend data and, 72–73; formative nature of, 72; funding analysis and, 74; issues in, 71–72; multidimensional nature of, 71–72; policy analysis and, 72; program director interviews and, 73–74; program manager study and, 73; qualitative approach to, 72; quantitative approach to, 72; state policy context of, 71; systemic outcomes of, 72; user group discussions and, 75

State government: barriers to services integration by, 69; local services delivery and, 69–70; policy-organization-centered approach and, 70; services evaluation issues and, 71–72

Strategic Plan for Families and Children (Colo.), 70, 76

Training: CISS projects and, 45; service delivery model and, 14

U.S. Department of Education, 8, 48

U.S. Department of Health, Education, and Welfare (HEW), 6, 7

Vandergrift, J. A., 11

View, V. A., 36, 48

Wagner, M., 63

Wasik, B. H., 36, 37, 38, 41, 42, 44, 46

Wehlage, G., 23

Weiss, C. H., 26, 87, 94

Weiss, H. G., 5, 22, 26, 31

White, K. R., 30

White, W. A., 23, 54

Wingspread Conference, 6, 8, 13, 15

Woolverton, S., 26

Yin, R. K., 45

Young, N., 69

ORDERING INFORMATION

NEW DIRECTIONS FOR EVALUATION is a series of paperback books that presents the latest techniques and procedures for conducting useful evaluation studies of all types of programs. Books in the series are published quarterly in Spring, Summer, Fall, and Winter and are available for purchase by subscription as well as by single copy.

SUBSCRIPTIONS for 1996 cost $59.00 for individuals (a savings of 22 percent over single-copy prices) and $87.00 for institutions, agencies, and libraries. Please do not send institutional checks for personal subscriptions. Standing orders are accepted. (For subscriptions outside of North America, add $7.00 for shipping via surface mail or $25.00 for air mail. Orders *must be prepaid* in U.S. dollars by check drawn on a U.S. bank or charged to VISA, MasterCard, or American Express.)

SINGLE COPIES cost $19.00 plus shipping (see below) when payment accompanies order. California, New Jersey, New York, and Washington, D.C., residents please include appropriate sales tax. Canadian residents add GST and any local taxes. Billed orders will be charged shipping and handling. No billed shipments to post office boxes. (Orders from outside North America *must be prepaid* in U.S. dollars by check drawn on a U.S. bank or charged to VISA, MasterCard, or American Express.)

SHIPPING (SINGLE COPIES ONLY): $10.00 and under, add $2.50; to $20.00, add $3.50; to $50.00, add $4.50; to $75.00, add $5.50; to $100.00, add $6.50; to $150.00, add $7.50; over $150.00, add $8.50.

DISCOUNTS FOR QUANTITY ORDERS are available. Please write to the address below for information.

ALL ORDERS must include either the name of an individual or an official purchase order number. Please submit your order as follows:
   Subscriptions: specify series and year subscription is to begin
   Single copies: include individual title code (such as PE59)

MAIL ALL ORDERS TO:
   Jossey-Bass Publishers
   350 Sansome Street
   San Francisco, California 94104-1342

FOR SUBSCRIPTION SALES OUTSIDE OF THE UNITED STATES, CONTACT:
   any international subscription agency or Jossey-Bass directly.

OTHER TITLES AVAILABLE IN THE
NEW DIRECTIONS FOR EVALUATION SERIES
Lois-ellin G. Datta, Editor-in-Chief

PE68   Reasoning in Evaluation: Inferential Links and Leaps, *Deborah M. Fournier*
PE67   Evaluating Country Development Policies and Programs: New Approaches
        for a New Agenda, *Robert Picciotto, Ray C. Rist*
PE66   Guiding Principles for Evaluators, *William R. Shadish, Dianna L. Newman,
        Mary Ann Scheirer, Christopher Wye*
PE65   Emerging Roles of Evaluation in Science Education Reform,
        Rita G. O'Sullivan
PE64   Preventing the Misuse of Evaluation, *Carla J. Stevens, Micah Dial*
PE63   Critically Evaluating the Role of Experiments, *Kendon J. Conrad*
PE62   The Preparation of Professional Evaluators: Issues, Perspectives, and Pro-
        grams, *James W. Altschuld, Molly Engle*
PE61   The Qualitative-Quantitative Debate: New Perspectives, *Charles S. Reichardt,
        Sharon E. Rallis*
PE60   Program Evaluation: A Pluralistic Enterprise, *Lee Sechrest*
PE59   Evaluating Chicago School Reform, *Richard P. Niemiec, Herbert J. Walberg*
PE58   Hard-Won Lessons in Program Evaluation, *Michael Scriven*
PE57   Understanding Causes and Generalizing About Them, *Lee B. Sechrest,
        Anne G. Scott*
PE56   Varieties of Investigative Evaluation, *Nick L. Smith*
PE55   Evaluation in the Federal Government: Changes, Trends, and Opportunities,
        Christopher G. Wye, Richard C. Sonnichsen
PE54   Evaluating Mental Health Services for Children, *Leonard Bickman,
        Debra J. Rog*
PE53   Minority Issues in Program Evaluation, *Anna-Marie Madison*
PE52   Evaluating Programs for the Homeless, *Debra J. Rog*
PE50   Multisite Evaluations, *Robin S. Turpin, James M. Sinacore*
PE49   Organizations in Transition: Opportunities and Challenges for Evaluation,
        Colleen L. Larson, Hallie Preskill
PE47   Advances in Program Theory, *Leonard Bickman*
PE45   Evaluation and Social Justice: Issues in Public Education, *Kenneth A. Sirotnik*
PE44   Evaluating Training Programs in Business and Industry,
        Robert O. Brinkerhoff
PE42   International Innovations in Evaluation Methodology, *Ross F. Conner,
        Michael Hendricks*
PE43   Evaluating Health Promotion Programs, *Marc T. Braverman*
PE41   Evaluation and the Federal Decision Maker, *Gerald L. Barkdoll,
        James B. Bell*
PE40   Evaluating Program Environments, *Kendon J. Conrad,
        Cynthia Roberts-Gray*
PE39   Evaluation Utilization, *John A. McLaughlin, Larry J. Weber,
        Robert W. Covert, Robert B. Ingle*
PE38   Timely, Lost-Cost Evaluation in the Public Sector, *Christopher G. Wye,
        Harry P. Hatry*
PE36   The Client Perspective on Evaluation, *Jeri Nowakowski*
PE35   Multiple Methods in Program Evaluation, *Melvin M. Mark,
        R. Lance Shotland*
PE33   Using Program Theory in Evaluation, *Leonard Bickman*
PE31   Advances in Quasi-Experimental Design and Analysis,
        William M. K. Trochim
PE30   Natur... .... David D. Williams